Historic
Plymouth

British Library Cataloguing in Publication Data
Trahair, Stephen
Historic Plymouth
1. Devon. Plymouth, history
1. Title
942.3'58

A catalogue record for this book is available from the British Library
ISBN 978-1-9160190-5-8

Design & Maps: Ben Robinson
© Stephen Trahair 2021

First published August 2021

Published by:
Pen & Ink Publishing
34 New Street, Barbican
Plymouth, PL1 2NA
01752 705337 | www.chrisrobinson.co.uk

Printed & bound in Great Britain by:
Short Run Press Limited
25 Bittern Road
Sowton Industrial Estate
Exeter, EX2 7LW
01392 211909 | www.shortrunpress.co.uk

While every effort has been made to contact copyright-holders
of material reproduced in this book, the publisher would be
glad to rectify in future editions any errors or omissions.

Front cover image and aerial Hoe views courtesy Wes Ashton

A short guide to the people, places and events of

Historic
Plymouth

Stephen Trahair

Pen&Ink

HISTORIC PLYMOUTH

I was born and brought up in West Devon, where Plymouth was just somewhere you went to school or work, or occasionally to the cinema. Plymouth seemed to me an alien place with little to commend it. But I've lived in Plymouth now for some years, and I love it. Often the best bits are hidden in unexpected places, and round every corner there is something to remind you that Plymouth has more history per square mile than anywhere else I know.

A settlement named Tamari Ostia (mouth of the Tamar) is listed in the Cosmographia made by the Greek cartographer Ptolemy in 150 AD, although its whereabouts is unknown. It was probably near Cremyll on the Cornish side, or at Stonehouse Creek on the Devon side.

Sutton Pool (otherwise known as Sutton Harbour) was the site of the original Bronze Age settlement called Billa's Burgh which became the City of Plymouth. The Manor of *Sudtone* (Sutton, meaning 'south farm or settlement' in Old English) is mentioned in the Norman Domesday Book of 1086 with a population of just 70 people, while the first reference to *Plimothe* (the place at the mouth of the Plym) is around 200 years later. In contrast, Plympton was already a borough town before the Norman Conquest.

Plymouth grew rapidly in the thirteenth and fourteenth centuries, so that by 1371 it was England's fourth largest town with around 7,000 inhabitants. In 1439 it became the first town to be incorporated by Royal Charter, and two centuries later it was the sixth biggest trading and fishing port in the country, although it was still huddled around the shores of Sutton Pool.

With the discovery of the Americas, Sutton Harbour found itself the main point of departure for the New World, a position it held until the development of Bristol and Liverpool in the nineteenth century. It would have been a familiar anchorage to all the Elizabethan explorers from Humphrey Gilbert and Walter Raleigh to Francis Drake, and was of course the port from which the *Mayflower* set sail with nonconformist émigrés in 1620, bound for the distant shores of Massachusetts.

When the Spanish Armada was sighted in 1588 and Drake led the English fleet to destroy it, it was from Sutton Harbour and the Cattewater that they set sail. The dockyard and port of Plymouth Dock - later Devonport - only came into existence in the late seventeenth century, although within 100 years the population of Devonport had outstripped that of Plymouth.

The twentieth century wrought immense change to the city centre, and the post-war rebuilding seemed to narrow the focus on the shopping streets which are its least interesting part. But in spite of the destruction of the 1940s and 50s, some part of that long and fascinating history lies everywhere in Plymouth – often hidden, sometimes difficult to recognise. The aim of this guidebook is to shine a light on those many things, both new and old, celebrated or neglected, of which Plymouth can boast.

I have not included those venues like the National Marine Aquarium or The Box which are already well-advertised. I have concentrated instead on places which are not so familiar.

The list of places referred to in this guidebook is inevitably a personal choice, and no doubt I have omitted to mention things which others would have included. I chose places about which I felt I had something interesting to say, and in particular those places which are associated with people. I have not written it just for antiquarians or local history buffs, but for anyone who wants to learn about the city, visitors and residents alike. I hope that there is something for everyone in these few pages.

The sketch plans for each section are for identification only, to give the approximate location of the places referred to. Not all the places are open to the public, and some are open by prior arrangement only.

Where I refer to activities you can take part in, please check whether and when they are available before visiting them, as things change year by year, and what is available when this goes to print may cease to be available later on.

ACKNOWLEDGEMENTS

This guidebook is not a work of scholarship, and in compiling it I have relied on many and varied sources. Those who seek original research from the archival sources should refer (as I have done) to the history books, in particular Crispin Gill's *Plymouth: a New History* [Devon Books, 1993] and Chris Robinson's *A History of Devonport* [Pen & Ink Publishing, 2010]. I also commend Felicity Goodall's *Lost Plymouth* [Birlinn Ltd, 2009] and Laura Quigley's *Bloody British History: Plymouth* [The History Press, 2012].

Particular thanks are due to Chris and Ben Robinson, Felicity Goodall and Paul Burkhalter for their advice and suggestions. I also acknowledge the help (among others) of Nigel Overton, Richard Fisher, Derek Tait and Thomas Jonglez, whose excellent Secret Guides to the great cities of the world inspired the format. I have made good use of the abundance of online sources available, as well as books, booklets and pamphlets. However, with 120 entries about entirely different places, people and events, it would take too long to acknowledge each and every source consulted, and I apologise to those whose work I have used in this way.

Finally, I have to acknowledge the encouragement provided by the lockdown following the Covid-19 outbreak in 2020, in prompting me to complete what I had started two years earlier.

Stephen Trahair 2021

CONTENTS

Historic
Plymouth

City Centre

1. The City Centre and Armada Way
2. Beckley Point, Coburg Street
3. Plymouth University Marine Institute, Coburg Street
4. Immersive Vision Theatre, Portland Square
5. Portland Square Memorial
6. Drake's Place, North Hill
7. Tudor Plymouth Mural, Eastlake Street
8. Ebrington Street
9. Tramway Junction Box, Beaumont Road
10. Telephone Exchange, Eastlake Ope
11. Bank Building, St Andrew's Cross
12. Drake Scratching, St Andrew's Minster
13. Prysten House, Finewell Street

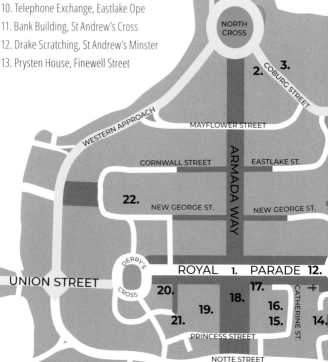

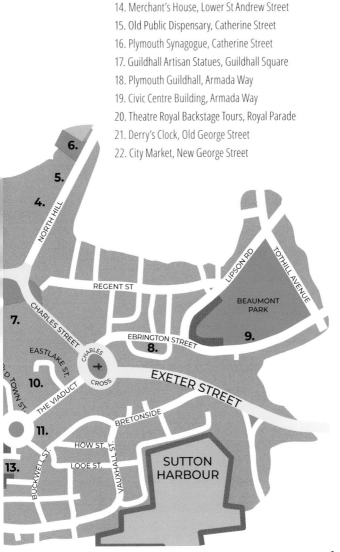

1. THE CITY CENTRE AND ARMADA WAY

The first city to plan for post-war reconstruction and a new centre

In March and April 1941 the heart of Plymouth was destroyed in a series of devastating air-raids which left the city in ruins. In total, there were 59 raids on Plymouth during the Second World War which killed 1,172 civilians and caused 4,448 casualties, the highest proportion per capita of any British city. The bombs destroyed nearly 4,000 houses, 26 schools, 41 churches and the administrative and shopping centres of Plymouth and Devonport.

But the city carried on. Even before the bombs had stopped falling, plans were in place to design a new city centre, and as early as 1943 the Plan for Plymouth was drawn up by an eminent town planner, Professor Patrick Abercrombie, assisted by the City Engineer, James Paton Watson. It was approved by the council in 1944. The Plymouth Plan was the most radical and ambitious scheme of reconstruction in the country, creating what has been described as 'the first and last great Beaux-Arts city plan in Britain'.

Plymouth was also the first British city to commence rebuilding, and by 1951 the remains of the old centre had been cleared away and the first buildings erected along Royal Parade, New George Street, Old Town Street and Armada Way. The design of these buildings – the main ones being E Dingle & Co, John Yeo's, Spooners, Pophams, Lloyds Bank, Prudential Assurance - was rigorously controlled, and can best be seen in Royal Parade: large blocks faced in white Portland stone with framed 'picture' windows and a few decorative elements, a rather bland marriage of classicism and modernism contrasting with green avenues of trees.

The Plan for Plymouth involved demolishing a number of buildings which had survived the war, many of historic importance. This chimed with the mood of the time, when voters embraced Labour's plans for a National Health Service, welfare provision and nationalised utilities, rejecting Churchill's conservatism. People wanted to sweep away the old and make a fresh start, building a New Britain to bring hope for the future. The bombed-out shell of Charles Church was scheduled for destruction, but in the event was retained, marooned in the middle of a roundabout, a monument to the horrors of civilian bombardment.

Both the picture opposite and on page vii show Armada Way, the wide pedestrian boulevard which cuts a swathe through the pre-war centre from North Cross to The Hoe. The earlier picture, taken from the Plan, looks north from a roundabout in Royal Parade which was never built, and shows how Abercrombie envisaged the city would look. Although his architectural ambitions were never fully realised, he and Paton Watson have nevertheless left Plymouth with a period piece, the most complete 1950s civic landscape in Britain.

When in 1941 a school-mistress pinned a board with the word *Resurgam* ('I will rise again') above the north door of the burnt-out St Andrew's Minster, it was for the church she loved. But the city rose again too, a newer and – yes, for all its faults – a better city.

2. BECKLEY POINT, NORTH CROSS

Plymouth's tallest building at 256 feet

Completed in 2017, Beckley Point towers above the city from the highest point in the central area, and can be seen ahead of you in the distance as you approach Plymouth along the A38. But who was 'Beckley' and why is the building named after him?

John Henry Beckly (spelt thus) was a wealthy Plymouth businessman who ran the well-known department store of John Yeo, and was one of the city's principal benefactors in the first half of the twentieth century. He was a strong Methodist and a keen social reformer. His obituary in the Western Independent following his death in December 1932 described him as someone who "could not live without sharing the good fortune which his business acumen brought to him, and his benevolence was probably the keenest joy in his life".

He left a total of £20,000 to various Plymouth charities and churches (the purchasing power of £20,000 is now around £5m). There were substantial legacies to Plymouth YMCA, the St John's Ambulance Service and King Street Methodist Church. A sum of £10,000 was given to establish the Beckly Trust "for the benefit of such of the neediest children of Plymouth as are crippled, sick or otherwise disabled", and the Trust is still active in helping to meet those needs. He also left equally substantial sums to Shebbear College and other Wesleyan colleges.

His nephew, William Edwin Beckly, continued the Beckly family's involvement with the YMCA and John Yeo's department store from 1933 and into the 1970s. It fell to him to find alternative premises for John Yeo's during the Blitz when the old store was destroyed, and to keep the business going as best he could. After the war an imposing new YMCA building was erected at the junction of Armada Way and Coburg Street, which was sold for student accommodation in the 1990s when it ceased to be used for its original purpose. It was named Beckly Court in recognition of Edwin Beckly's dedication to the work of the YMCA for so many years.

Recently Beckly Court was sold and demolished for the construction of Beckley Point. The alteration in the spelling of 'Beckly' seems to have occurred because of a typographical error. Although the postal address and registered title of Beckly Court gave the correct spelling, the name of the holding company did not, and it appears that the new owners, the Student Housing Company, adopted the misspelling.

Edwin Beckly was my grandfather. He was a true Devonian: a home-loving and kindly man, who never lost his slow Devon burr and avoided the limelight. He would have been astonished to learn that the tallest building in the region, visible from so many of the approaches to the city, is named after him.

3. PLYMOUTH UNIVERSITY MARINE INSTITUTE

Plymouth's international standing in marine biology and maritime research

Whatever aspect of the sea you can think of – marine biology and ecosystems, marine engineering, harbour design and management, pollution with micro-plastics, renewable energy, hydrography, coastal erosion, wave movement, ocean forecasting - Plymouth is at the forefront of international research and innovation. Researchers from Plymouth University's Marine Institute, the Marine Biological Association, the Sir Alister Hardy Foundation for Ocean Science, and Plymouth Marine Laboratory are active across the globe, from the Bahamas to the Solomon Islands and from the USA to Japan.

Plymouth Sound and the Western English Channel have been continually monitored for longer than any other maritime area on earth. Investigations into its marine life, geology and tidal movements have been carried out since 1888, providing an invaluable source of data covering a period of major environmental change, and which has led to many important advances in our understanding of the marine environment.

These investigations have been undertaken by the Marine Biological Association (opened in 1884 and based under the walls of the Citadel), which has been in the forefront of research into all aspects of marine life. Ground-breaking research into how nerve cells communicate with each other using the giant axons found in squid, led to our modern understanding of the nervous system. The MBA is also home to the Sir Alister Hardy Foundation for Ocean Science which now manages the Continuous Plankton Recorder survey started in 1931, the longest running and most geographically extensive marine ecological survey in the world.

Plymouth University's new £19m Marine Building houses a major wave energy testing tank and a simulator, enabling students to train in piloting vessels of all sizes from yachts to supertankers. The university undertakes research and training in subjects as diverse as marine science and technology, maritime business, logistics and port management, and marine art.

Plymouth is also home to the Plymouth Marine Laboratory, a charity whose aim is to develop and apply innovative marine science to ensure a sustainable future for the world's oceans, and to the National Marine Aquarium, whose Atlantic Ocean tank is the deepest in the UK, with 2.5 million litres of water.

Oceansgate is a new Marine Business Technology centre based in what was the South Yard of Devonport Dockyard, where there will be a unique complex of industrial buildings, jetties and dry docks, with direct access to the English Channel and to a marine testing area for autonomous vehicles and electronic sensor systems.

4. IMMERSIVE VISION THEATRE, UNIVERSITY

A mini-planetarium with a story to tell

Plymouth University's Immersive Vision Theatre (IVT) was built in 1967 by Plymouth Polytechnic as the William Day Planetarium. In 2008 it was completely transformed using 'full-dome architecture', with images generated digitally through a high-resolution projector fitted with a fish-eye lens and connected to customised computers. Audiences can be flown through the Milky Way to galaxies far, far away, and travel deep into the human body to the microscopic and even nanoscopic level. Plymouth is one of very few universities to have such a facility at its disposal.

Using data from NASA and the European Space Agency, the IVT is enhancing students' learning about everything from particle physics to the geology on the surface of Mars. It is also regularly used by the Plymouth Astronomical Society, and even by local cubs and scouts to earn their astronomy badges.

On 18 December 1984 an article in The Times described a remarkable event at the planetarium which appeared to pinpoint the exact date of Christ's birth in Bethlehem: 15 September in the year 7 BC. Dr Percy Seymour was an astronomer at what was then Plymouth Polytechnic, who became interested in the mystery of the Star of Bethlehem which brought the Wise Men to Judea. St Matthew's Gospel describes them as having predicted the birth of 'one born to be king of the Jews' from the rising of a great star. Using published data on the movement of the planets 2,000 years ago he recreated the night sky over Bethlehem. He had to rewind the clock back to 7 BC before anything dramatic appeared, but was amazed when a huge star appeared on the planetarium screen on what would now be 15 September. This proved to be formed by an unusually close conjunction of the planets Saturn and Jupiter in the constellation of Pisces.

The planets are among the brightest objects in the night sky, and Jupiter is the fourth brightest object visible from the Earth. With Jupiter eclipsing Saturn, Saturn's rings and its diffracted light would have doubled its light intensity.

The Wise Men (the 'Three Kings' or Magi) would have been astrologers, who studied the stars in order to predict earthly events, and were remarkably knowledgeable about the movements of the planets and constellations. For them, such a conjunction would have been associated with the birth of a king of the Jews, since Jupiter was the planet of Kings, Saturn the protector of the Jews, and Pisces was the zodiac sign associated with Palestine.

"When our calendar was revised in the Middle Ages it is possible that some mistakes were made in the calculations, and that we have been celebrating Christmas on the wrong date and seven years late for something like 500 years," Dr Seymour said. "But I will continue to celebrate Christmas Day on the 25 December like everyone else."

5. PORTLAND SQUARE MEMORIAL

Site of a wartime air-raid shelter destroyed during the Blitz of 1941

On 22 April 1941 the sirens wailed to signal yet another imminent air raid on Plymouth, and those without their own place of safety hurried to the nearest air-raid shelter, marshalled by the ARP wardens.

Many people would have had an Anderson shelter, a corrugated iron structure with a curved roof which was buried in their garden. They provided effective protection against a blast from a nearby explosion, but they were rather claustrophobic and prone to flooding, and in wet or cold weather were miserable places to spend a night. An alternative design was introduced in 1941 known as the Morrison shelter, a steel table with space beneath for two people to sleep. This was designed to protect the occupants from the partial collapse of the house. Others simply crouched in an understairs cupboard.

In the North Hill area where the university campus now stands was Portland Square, an elegant Victorian square surrounding a small park under which a shelter had been built with room for 280 people. This was arch-roofed and designed with many right-angle corners to reduce the effect of blast in the event of a direct hit. Escape hatches were provided to enable people to evacuate the shelter if the entrances were blocked.

The Plymouth & District Deaf & Dumb Institute was at No.3 Portland Square and by the time the patients had been roused and dressed, the nearest entrance to the shelter was full, so many of them had to make their way around the square to the north east entrance.

It is not known how many people were in the shelter when the bombs started to fall, or how many died when a direct hit by a German bomb destroyed the north east section. The figure is believed to be between 72 and 76, but the blast was so strong that some people were simply vaporised, and body parts were left hanging from the trees. This was the single worst tragedy to befall the civilian population of Plymouth during the Second World War. Whole families lost their lives, but many more were protected from blast by the design of the shelter.

The chaplain of the Deaf Institute wrote a prayer for the comfort of the remaining patients when the bombs fell once more: "Lord keep us safe at night, secure from all our fears; may angels guard us while we sleep, till morning light appears."

In 2012 construction work at Plymouth University uncovered one of the entrances to the shelter, enabling a photographic record to be made of the interior, which was surprisingly intact. It is likely that the damage to the shelter was repaired so that it could function once more, giving such comfort as its narrow, dark and claustrophobic tunnels could provide.

6. DRAKE'S PLACE, NORTH HILL

Former Plymouth reservoir fed by water from Drake's Leat

In 1585 an 'Acte for ye Presvacon of ye Haven of Plymowth' was obtained by the Mayor and Corporation, to bring water from the headwaters of the River Meavy on Dartmoor down to Plymouth by means of an open channel or leat. Before work could start, relations with Spain deteriorated and most of the city's labourers were enlisted in the war which culminated in the Spanish Armada of 1588, so it was not until 1590 that work began in earnest.

Sir Francis Drake had been instrumental in assisting the Bill's passage through Parliament, and Drake was appointed to carry out the work. He was paid the grand sum of £300 to cover both the cost of the work and the compensation paid to the landowners across whose land the leat passed. The work progressed quickly (the leat was originally just a rough ditch, although considerable engineering skill was required to ensure an even gradient) and by 1591 fresh water was flowing to Plymouth.

Drake's Leat, as it came to be called (somewhat ambiguously named 'Sir Francis Drake's Water' on a map of 1643), ended at a reservoir or tank somewhere in the vicinity of Drake's Place, from which water was supplied to the townspeople via lead pipes and gutters to 27 'conduit houses' around the town. The inscription on the Old Town Conduit ("Made in the Maioraltie of John Trelawnye 1598") is preserved in the exterior wall of Drake's Place. The leat also supplied water to power a number of mills, including one owned by Drake where these gardens now stand.

The present reservoir at Drake's Place was built in 1825, and was the main source of water for the town before new reservoirs were constructed at Hartley and Crownhill. In 1898 Burrator Reservoir was built at the head of the Meavy valley near Dousland, replacing the simple weir which now lies deep beneath its surface, and water reached Plymouth via pipes rather than open leats for the first time.

Drake's Place was home to George Frean, who went into partnership with Mr Peek in 1857 to form the famous biscuit makers Peek Frean & Co Ltd, manufacturers of Garibaldis, Bourbons and Twiglets. In the 1880s the mills and houses at Drake's Place were demolished and replaced by the present gardens, which opened in 1891, including a broad promenade alongside the reservoir over a colonnade of granite pillars believed to be from Plymouth's old covered market.

In 2007 Plymouth University took over the lease for the gardens and reservoir from Plymouth City Council, and major work was undertaken to restore the gardens and open the Reservoir Café, which opened in 2014.

Drake left his mark on Plymouth in many ways, and we will meet him several times during the course of this guide.

7. TUDOR PLYMOUTH MURAL, EASTLAKE ST

A bird's eye view of Plymouth in Tudor times

This ceramic mural near the Eastlake Street entrance to Drake Circus Shopping Mall was made by Philippa Threlfall, and was officially unveiled by HRH Princess Anne when the previous Drake Circus complex was opened in 1971. This was a featureless modular concrete development which looked as if it was designed by a quantity surveyor, and its demolition after only 35 years or so was met with general relief. The mural had been displayed in an underpass, and is the only good thing to have survived from that monument to unloveliness.

The mural design is based on several different maps, including a Henry VIII map of Plymouth now in the British Museum (below), a 1660s plan by Sir Bernard de Gomme (the engineer in charge of the Royal Citadel fortification), and a 1765 map of the city by Benjamin Donn. The mural shows prominent buildings and churches, and sheep grazing on the Hoe. The fortifications are there, with the chain which could be stretched across the mouth of Sutton Pool and raised when the enemy approached. Small ferry boats ply their trade and ships' sails billow with the westerly wind. Farmers till the soil around the gibbet at Teat's Hill, and a great fish swims near the towers of Plympton Priory.

Each small house was made as a separate piece of ceramic, giving it a mosaic-like quality. The churches and religious houses have windows filled with melted red, blue or green glass, forming points of colour among the earthy tones of the houses. The texture and glazes of the fields and orchards add to the richness of the design.

8. EBRINGTON STREET

Plymouth's only surviving pre–war city centre street

Ebrington Street reminds us what much of Plymouth's city centre was like before the Second World War: two or three storey buildings mostly from the nineteenth century, narrow streets, and small traders. The street runs west from Beaumont Park on a slightly winding route past shops, houses, pubs and cafes, with numerous side streets and a zebra crossing, until suddenly it all falls away, and the post-war inner bypass cuts us off from Drake Circus shopping mall and the modern city centre.

Ebrington Street was one of the main commercial thoroughfares of the late 19th and early twentieth century city, although before the last war the street was called Ham Street, and Ebrington Street started more or less where it now ends. It has a number of fine old buildings including the late Victorian 'Bread and Roses' pub (formerly the 'Trafalgar') and an elegant Regency town-house set back from the shopfronts and easy to miss. Ebrington Street has recently acquired something hipsterish about it, with a varied selection of cafes, bistros and independent shops, and a vibrant student community.

There is much to see of interest. Chief among them is the fine shopfront surmounted by the word 'Cinedrome', which has recently been restored to its Edwardian style. The Cinedrome, one of Plymouth's many pre-war cinemas, opened its doors in 1911, advertising a 'magnificent' series of programmes with "dainty afternoon teas served free". Silent cine film was shown, accompanied by a small orchestra, and the opening night included several short films including an instructive series of pictures showing the habits of insects. In 1916 the management proudly proclaimed that the first cinema organ in the city (specially built for the Cinedrome) had been installed. The advent of 'talkies' in the late 1920s was frowned on by the proprietors, and in October 1929 the Cinedrome was advising sternly that "Talkies are NOT screened here, only the best silent films, accompanied by a human symphony orchestra under the direction of Mr Albert Hosie, late of the Savoy". The film being shown at the time was *Does Mother Know Best?*

The Cinedrome was badly damaged in the Blitz in 1941 and the 900-seat auditorium was demolished. Fortunately the frontage survived.

Gould's, an army surplus and outdoor clothing store founded in the 1900s, moved there in 1955. Gould's was the sort of place where you could get pretty much anything military, and you wouldn't be surprised to hear the assistants behind the glass-topped counters saying, "Ethel, where did you put the AK47s?" "I think they're in the third drawer down, dear". It had an eclectic mix of unusual outdoor clothing, equipment and footwear, with some militaria from the Second World War and even the Warsaw Pact. One Trip Advisor reviewer thought it looked like the set for a Mervyn Peake novel.

Sadly it closed in 2020.

9. TRAMWAY JUNCTION BOX, BEAUMONT ROAD

Britain's first urban tram system

There are many old tramwire posts dotted around Plymouth, with their distinctive pointed finials. Most are now used as lamp-posts. They remind us that Plymouth was the first city in Britain to take advantage of the Tramways Act 1870, which made it easier to finance and build street tramways. The Plymouth, Stonehouse & Devonport Tramway was completed in 1872, and ran from Derry's Clock (behind the Theatre Royal) along Union Street, over Stonehouse Bridge and on to Devonport. It used horse-drawn trams.

The second company, the Plymouth, Devonport & District Tramways Company, was established in 1882 to build a 10 mile network running as far to the east as Plympton, but the directors were over-ambitious, and of the seven routes authorised only two were built. An injunction was obtained by Devonport Corporation preventing the company operating any services until the whole of the system was complete, and as the directors could not raise sufficient capital to do so, the company was sold to a new Plymouth Tramways Company in 1886.

The new company decided to use steam locomotives instead of horses, the directors assuming that Board of Trade approval for the use of steam would be a formality. Unfortunately approval was not forthcoming, and the actions of the directors resulted in the landmark ruling of Derry v Peek in 1889, familiar to lawyers from their law exams, which defined the tort of fraudulent misrepresentation. The 'Derry' referred to was William Derry, the Mayor of Plymouth after whom Derry's Cross is named.

Horse-trams were steadily replaced by electric trams drawing power from overhead wires, the last being converted in 1907. The last line to be built, the Devonport & District Tramways Co Ltd in 1901, used electric traction from the start. A junction box marked 'Plymouth Corporation Tramways' and dated 1899 can be seen in a wall in Beaumont Road.

In 1914 the 'three towns' of Plymouth, Stonehouse and Devonport were merged to form the Borough of Plymouth, and Plymouth Corporation later acquired the various tram companies that had previously operated independently. A tram depot and offices were built at Milehouse. From 1920 motor buses were introduced on new routes beyond the existing tram system, and during the 1930s motor buses began to replace trams as they reached the end of their working lives. The last remaining tram route, from the City Centre to Milehouse via Peverell, struggled on during the war despite the disruption caused by bomb damage to the track and the electrical supply, but finally closed in September 1945.

Although two of the three old tram sheds at the Milehouse depot have sadly been demolished recently, the words 'Plymouth Corporation Tramway Offices' are still displayed on the imposing 1922 façade of the Plymouth Citybus offices.

10. TELEPHONE EXCHANGE, EASTLAKE WALK

The women who carried on through the Blitz

Plymouth's Art Deco Telephone Exchange was completed in 1933. Now hidden behind other buildings and not easy to find, it is one of only a handful of pre-war buildings in the city centre that still serve the function for which they were built.

From the 1930s to the present day, the country's telephone system has been an essential part of everyday life which we take for granted, like the postal service. But during the war years it was especially important. The city's essential services, the military and government departments, had to be able to communicate with each other if the country was not to collapse into chaos, and maintaining and repairing the telephone lines and exchanges was a top priority.

At Exeter during the Blitz, twelve members of the Post Office staff were trapped in the basement telegraph office with the surrounding buildings in flames and the Post Office above them a furnace. The doors of the emergency exits glowed red-hot. Nevertheless, the staff pressed on with the despatch of urgent messages, and managed from time to time to keep Bristol informed of their situation. They all survived, thanks to the Post Office's contingency plans for emergencies.

The devastating raids on Plymouth in March 1941 virtually wiped out the whole of the city centre. Although surrounded by a sea of fire and destruction covering fifteen acres, the telephone exchange building escaped serious damage, and work carried on. The Devonport Telephone Exchange was completely destroyed, but Post Office engineers were on the road before daybreak, carrying out a pre-arranged scheme for restoring vital defence communication services, while others repaired breaks in the cables in the numerous craters on the road. Well, you had to just keep going, didn't you? There was a war on.

11. BANK BUILDING, ST ANDREW'S CROSS

The landmark bank building of the new city centre

In the aftermath of the Second World War the National Provincial Bank, along with the other major banking corporations, demonstrated its commitment to contemporary architecture with a series of new buildings, the most important being that at Plymouth. This building was to be the Bank's headquarters for South West England, and accordingly the chief architect, BC Sherren, was given a generous budget which is reflected in the quality of the decorative materials used.

St Andrew's Cross at the top end of the new Royal Parade was the most prominent and desirable of the post-war building sites. The bank, with its fine clock tower, remains one of the most important of Plymouth's 1950s Beaux Arts buildings. The design, with its pillared portico, is pure '50s classicism, with a curved copper-clad roof echoing that of the 1951 Royal Festival Hall, London. It opened in 1958.

The Grade II listing describes it as "an inventive re-working of traditional bank architecture, rationalising Classical forms to create a commanding building in which an impression of solidity is combined with spacious modernity", and commends it for its "high-quality materials, including granite and internal stone cladding, with bronze windows, balustrades and handrails, as well as the integration of artistic features such as mosaic, worked bronze doors, and sandblasted glass."

The blue wall within the portico is decorated with turquoise mosaic, with designs in gold drawn from the histories of both the bank and Plymouth. The two great bronze doors (which are not used) have decorative roundels depicting coins through the ages.

From its curved copper roof rises an illuminated clock tower with blue glass panels, surmounted by a crow's nest with a bronze balustrade and flag-pole. The clock lantern and the chamber beneath it contain the original clock with its working machinery.

The National Provincial Bank became part of the National Westminster Bank in 1970, which was in turn absorbed into the Royal Bank of Scotland in 2000. The building is no longer used as a bank branch, though a small section of the former banking hall is used for business banking, with office space above. Much of the building is empty.

The change of use has led to unsightly modifications to the original Banking Hall, and the exterior currently has a rather uncared-for look. The fine bronze doors are covered with peeling paint, and the windows are dirty. To maintain such a prominent city centre building in this state does not reflect well on the Royal Bank of Scotland.

12. DRAKE SCRATCHING, ST ANDREW'S MINSTER

Was this a doodle by Sir Francis Drake?

On the south side of the nave of St Andrew's Minster, on the sloping sill beneath one of the windows, is the Drake Scratching. This was found in about 1957 when the church was being restored after destruction by fire in the Blitz, and a piece of plaster was removed, revealing a sketch scratched into the plaster underneath. It shows what is clearly a globe representing the Earth and a sailing vessel with a line from its prow encircling it.

Between 1577 and 1580 Drake undertook an extremely arduous but highly profitable circumnavigation of the world in the *Pelican* (together with five other ships and a total of 164 men), rounding Cape Horn to reach the Pacific, sailing north as far as what is now California on the west coast of the Americas, crossing the Pacific to reach Indonesia, and returning via the Cape of Good Hope. While in the Pacific he captured two Spanish treasure ships laden with large quantities of gold.

On 26 September 1580 the now-renamed *Golden Hinde*, the only vessel to survive the journey intact, sailed into Plymouth with Drake and 59 remaining crew, along with a rich cargo of spices and captured Spanish treasure. Queen Elizabeth's half-share of this loot is said to have exceeded in value her entire annual income. Drake's was only the second successful circumnavigation of the globe after that of Magellan and Elcano in 1522, and six months later he was knighted on the deck of the *Golden Hinde* at Deptford, before a large crowd of admirers who had come to see England's most famous man, and now one of its wealthiest.

His official coat of arms was "Sable, a fess wavy between two pole-stars [Arctic and Antarctic] argent; and for his crest, a ship on a globe under ruff, held by a cable with a hand out of the clouds; over it this motto, *Auxilio Divino* [With the help of God]; underneath, *Sic Parvis Magna* [Great deeds come from small things]."

A feature of the coat of arms is the rope from the bow of the ship extending around the globe and into the hand of God. The scratching on the plaster at St Andrew's dates from around the late 1500s and is thought to be a doodle made by Drake, perhaps when discussing with some friends what might be a suitable design for his coat of arms. In later years Drake adopted the arms of the Drakes of Ash in East Devon, with whom he claimed kinship, in place of the somewhat elaborate armorial design granted by Queen Elizabeth, and perhaps first drafted on this window ledge.

Drake is not buried here. His last voyage to the Spanish Main (Caribbean), in 1595 with his cousin John Hawkins, proved a fiasco and both succumbed to fever. Drake was buried at sea off Porto Bello in 1596.

St Andrew's Minster has many fine monuments, and some striking post-war stained glass windows designed by John Piper.

13. PRYSTEN HOUSE AND THE DOOR OF UNITY

Plymouth's oldest dwelling house dating from the 1490s

O pposite the south door of St Andrew's Minster lies the Prysten House, built around 1498 for a wealthy Plymouth merchant, Thomas Yogge. How it came to be known as the Prysten House or 'house of priests' is unclear, since it appears it was never a priest's house or friary. The house is U-shaped, with an inner courtyard. It is owned by the City Council and is not currently open to the public, apart from the restaurant in the lower floor.

Beside the door leading into it from the south churchyard is a memorial to Captain William Allen and Midshipman Richard Delphey of the US Navy, who died from their wounds following a celebrated ship-to-ship duel between the USS *Argus* and HMS *Pelican* in 1813 during the so-called 'War of 1812' between Britain and the fledgling United States of America.

Under Captain Allen's command the 19-gun brig *Argus* (a 2-masted vessel, smaller than a frigate) was operating in the general area between Britain and Ireland, and by August 1813 had taken six British merchant ships. Lacking the crew to send any more captured ships to American or French ports as prizes, a further 21 captured merchant ships were set on fire. The cargo from these was worth about $2 million, a colossal sum in 1813, and the Admiralty sent all available ships to the area to hunt down the *Argus*.

On the morning of 14 August 1813 the 19-gun brig HMS *Pelican* spotted a plume of smoke 15 miles to the west of St David's Head off the Welsh coast, which proved to be from the most recent of the *Argus*' captured merchant ships to be set ablaze. Captain Allen could have evaded battle, as the *Argus* was less well-armed than the *Pelican* and was also faster, but he considered US seamanship was superior to British, and had boasted that he could "take any British 22-gun sloop-of-war in ten minutes". But after a brief but bloody battle, during which Captain Allen lost a leg to a cannonball and his first lieutenant was badly wounded, the US ship surrendered.

The captured *Argus* and her surviving crew were brought into Plymouth, where Captain Allen and the rest of the wounded were given medical attention, but he died on 18 August. He was given a funeral with full naval honours. His cortege was led by two companies of Royal Marines and a Guard of Honour, and the coffin (draped with the American flag) was carried by no less than eight Royal Navy captains. The officers and crew of the *Argus*, with officers of the Royal Marines and Army and non-combatants, followed behind. After a funeral at St Andrew's, Captain Allen was buried in the south churchyard. Midshipman Delphey had been buried the previous day, after losing both legs and succumbing to gangrene.

The Door of Unity was so named in 1930 following a generous donation from the USA towards the renovation of the Prysten House.

14. MERCHANT'S HOUSE, ST ANDREW STREET

Plymouth's best-preserved Elizabethan building, home of William Parker

The Merchant's House is a fine example of an Elizabethan dwelling-house. It was built by William Parker, a close friend and colleague of Francis Drake.

Parker was, like Drake, a privateer, a respected merchant and a one-time mayor. He served under Drake in 1588 in the fight against the Spanish Armada, and is thought to have commanded a vessel named the Mary Rose (a successor to the famous warship of Henry VIII which sank ignominiously in the Solent in 1545).

In 1601, on one of his privateering cruises, Parker captured a pair of Spanish treasure ships laden with 10,000 gold ducats, worth over £1m at today's gold price. On his return to Plymouth he used the profits from this to remodel an older house on this site into a fashionable timber-framed house. He helped promote the Plymouth Company to colonise North America, and took an active interest in the Virginia Colony. He died in 1618 on a voyage to the East Indies.

It is sometimes said that privateers were merely pirates, and 'El Draco' is said to be regarded as a pirate by the Spanish. However, this is to misunderstand the nature of warfare in the sixteenth century. Nations did not keep permanent armed forces as they do now. Armies and navies were assembled as the need arose, mostly using ships and men provided by the Lords of the Manor. Privateer vessels were privately-owned warships operating under a Letter of Marque, a royal licence authorising a named ship to take action against the king's enemies and naming the country whose ships could legally be taken as prizes.

A commissioned privateer enjoyed the protection of the laws of war and, if captured, the crew was entitled to be treated honourably as prisoners of war. Any actions which were not taken strictly in accordance with the Letter of Marque made a privateer a mere pirate, liable to be hung. Seeking enemy prizes under a Letter of Marque was considered an honourable and patriotic activity.

The Merchant's House was bought by Plymouth City Council in 1970 and restored. It is among the largest and finest surviving examples of a late sixteenth or early seventeenth century house in the country. The front room, where the family would entertain important guests, still features its huge original fireplace. It is currently closed, awaiting restoration.

Before closure, the seven rooms in the Merchant's House were themed to represent a distinct time period in Plymouth's history, covering topics such as transport, commerce, and the Second World War, with a room set aside to recreate the Blitz experience. One of the rooms was a replica of a Victorian schoolroom. Highlights of the historic objects on display included a 17th century carved mantelpiece, a Victorian dolls house, manacles used to detain prisoners and a ducking stool.

15. OLD PUBLIC DISPENSARY, CATHERINE STREET

One of the first charities providing free public health

The National Health Service which was set up by Attlee's Labour government after the Second World War provided a free health service for everyone, funded by the taxpayer. But it was not the first organisation making healthcare available to those who could not afford to pay for it. In the Middle Ages the poor were tended to by monks and nuns and there were almshouses in most towns established with the legacies of wealthy philanthropists to cater for the deserving elderly.

In the 1700s doctors were too expensive for most people and dealt only with the wealthiest members of society. Barber-surgeons were cheaper and capable of removing kidney stones, setting broken bones, or undertaking blood-letting, which was the remedy for a whole host of ailments and conditions. Apothecaries could prescribe traditional drugs and remedies. Otherwise, there were the itinerant quacks who peddled lotions and potions, powders and elixirs which were claimed to cure every ailment.

The development of industry with the Industrial Revolution of the late eighteenth and early nineteenth centuries brought many people into the slums and lodging houses of Plymouth seeking work and in these filthy and crowded tenements disease was rife. In the 1840s housing and public health in Plymouth was said to be worse than in any other European city apart from Warsaw. So much so that in 1852 the government commissioned a public enquiry into living conditions in Plymouth under Robert Rawlinson. He found that in Plymouth on average nine people lived in each dwelling, whereas the national average was only five or six. In Quarry Lane on the Barbican 50 to 60 people lived in one four-room house.

In 1798 the Plymouth Medical Society set up the Plymouth Public Dispensary, supported by voluntary subscriptions, to provide "gratuitous medical relief of poor persons who are unable to defray the expenses of procuring advice and medicines for themselves, and who are not in receipt of parish pay". This building in Catherine Street was opened in 1809 following a generous bequest by Dr Charles Yonge.

Plymouth's Public Dispensary was one of the very first organisations in Britain to make free healthcare available to those without the means to pay. In 1878 a subscription arrangement was started for those who could not afford private medical care but did not wish to accept charity, whereby they could pay a subscription – effectively a health insurance premium – to cover their healthcare needs. The monthly cost for a family with children under 14 was 1 shilling and 3 pence (about £4.50 today).

The organisation is still in existence, providing grants to Plymothians for the relief of suffering, although the Public Dispensary building was leased to the National Health Service from 1948 and is now used by the British Red Cross.

16. PLYMOUTH SYNAGOGUE, CATHERINE STREET

The oldest Ashkenazi synagogue in the English-speaking world

By the middle of the eighteenth century Plymouth had a well-established Jewish population. Many of them were members of the Emden family, who were Ashkenazi Jews from what is now Germany and the Netherlands. Ashkenazim are descended from Jews who settled along the Rhine before 1000 AD and adopted a unique way of life, blending traditions from Babylon, Judea and the Western Mediterranean with Germanic traditions. They spoke Yiddish, a mixture of German and other dialects.

Why the Emdens chose to settle in Plymouth is not clear. But by doing so, their descendants avoided the Holocaust under the Nazis which almost wiped out the Ashkenazi population on the Continent.

The synagogue was built in 1762, externally in a deliberately low-key style which is indistinguishable from many non-conformist chapels of the period. Jews kept a low profile in the eighteenth century. They were still subject to civil disability (as were Catholics) and were barred from public office, and had only limited property rights. The land on which the synagogue stands was leased in the name of a non-Jew, since leases signed by Jews were of doubtful validity. The two round-topped windows facing onto Catherine Street were only added in 1874 – prior to that date the synagogue presented a blank face to the street.

The entrance is around the back of the building, off a narrow passage (only open by prior appointment). The fine Baroque interior is in complete contrast to the bland exterior. The Torah Ark (the elaborate structure against the east wall) was probably made in Holland, shipped to Plymouth and then assembled in the synagogue. It is kept permanently lit. The Working Party on Jewish Monuments in the UK and Ireland stated in their 1999 publication that "...it is the only full-blooded Baroque Ark surviving in this country, complete with shadow painting of the Hebrew characters".

The Bimah (the central dais from which services are conducted) is believed to have been made by shipwrights from Devonport Dockyard, as the ornate woodturning and design are typical of eighteenth century naval joinery.

Apart from the stained glass windows and the extensions to the Ladies' Gallery along the north and south walls, the synagogue is unaltered from 1762, and even the candlesticks are the original ones.

Plymouth Synagogue is the oldest surviving synagogue in the UK apart from the Bevis Marks synagogue in London, built in 1701 by the Sephardim from Spain and Portugal.

17. GUILDHALL ARTISAN STATUES

Historic carved relief statues lining the north wall of the Guildhall

The Guildhall was designed by the Plymouth architects Norman & Hine, who had won a competition judged by Alfred Waterhouse, a famous London architect who was particularly associated with the Gothic Revival of the mid nineteenth century. It was completed in 1874.

The north side of the exterior, facing Royal Parade, has a row of twelve relief panels which fortunately survived the Blitz intact. These were made by a well-known sculptor, Richard Boulton of Cheltenham, and depict various artisans and allegorical figures in mediaeval costume. First we see a woman pointing with her right hand – blackened with soot and the patina of age – to a cross while holding a book, presumably the Bible although the inscription on it is obscure. Then we have a young man, perhaps a pilgrim, sitting with his hand on a lion's head while a very trusting lamb looks up at him; he sits near a beehive with his foot resting on a broken cannon. This is clearly an allegorical representation of words from chapter 11 of the Book of Isaiah, describing the peace of the Messianic age, when "they shall not hurt nor destroy in all my holy mountain".

Then in contrast we see a soldier in chain-mail with a shield and (now broken) sword, with the words from Shakespeare's Julius Caesar where Mark Antony swears vengeance on Caesar's assassins: "Cry havoc! Let loose the dogs of war". At his feet are a battle-axe and a spear. Next a sculptor carving a statue of a king, holding his mallet and chisel, followed by a musician playing a pipe organ of the type used in the Middle Ages. Then we have an artist sitting at his easel with brush and pallet.

The next figure is perhaps a master builder (or what we would now call an architect), using a pair of compasses to scale from a plan. To the modern eye he appears to be talking on his mobile, perhaps trying to pacify an impatient client. In the background there is a set-square and a campanile. Then we have an astronomer sitting on a pile of learned books while he peers through a telescope. His desk has an ink-pot.

Next we see a coppersmith or blacksmith wearing his leather apron, hammering a piece of metal on a stone anvil. Other tools including snips and a sharp-ended hammer are conveniently to hand, and around him are cog wheels with a geared belt-drive in the background.

Then we have a merchant sitting at his desk on a bale of wool, writing in his accounting book. He has a horn fixed to the side of his desk which serves as an inkwell. A trading ship can be seen behind him. Next a wealthy farmer holding a sheaf of wheat and a bunch of grapes, surrounded by fruits and sacks of flour. And finally what may be another allegorical picture, a heavily bearded figure holding a book and pointing with emphasis to the 'IX' in a column of Latin numerals.

18. PLYMOUTH GUILDHALL

Victorian gothic building transformed by 1950s styling

Between 1870 and 1874 Plymouth's growing importance was recognised by the construction of a new Guildhall and Municipal Building, forming two sides of a wide square with St Andrew's church tower at the east end. The Guildhall included an eastern wing comprising the City Treasury, and a western one containing council offices. The architectural style was high Victorian Gothic (then all the rage) complete with tall rather Bavarian-looking turrets.

The Guildhall and Municipal Building were both gutted by fire in 1940-1, apart from the City Treasury which survived the Blitz. The post-war Plan for Plymouth envisaged sweeping away the ruins and replacing them with new buildings in the 1950s Beaux Arts style. The Guildhall was saved from demolition by the vote of a single councillor in 1951 and, along with St Andrew's, was one of the few damaged buildings to be restored. The Municipal Building including the Law Courts was demolished, and its foundations lie beneath Royal Parade.

The interior of the Great Hall is a striking example of 1950s styling, with its shiny mahogany panelling, wedding-cake chandeliers, plaster reliefs in the ceiling by David Weeks depicting the Twelve Labours of Hercules, and new glazing in the original gothic windows depicting scenes from Plymouth's history made in 'sculpt-art', an experimental 1950s method involving diamond-cut images infilled with colour. The only anachronistic decorative element is the tapestry at the east end, a copy of Rafael's The Miraculous Draught of Fishes of 1519.

The building is Grade II listed for "the conservation of a 19th century Gothic building with new work that was entirely modern in spirit and redolent of the philosophy of the 1950s, and in its use and celebration of purely decorative art and in its slightly whimsical atmosphere, it is a rare and unusually rich example of an unaltered 'Festival of Britain' interior".

19. THE CIVIC CENTRE BUILDING

1960s design classic or an eyesore?

Few buildings in Plymouth have caused such controversy as the Civic Centre, when the council's plan to demolish it in 2007 was prevented by an eleventh hour listing by English Heritage. Architecture of the post-war period, and in particular that of the 1960s and 70s, represents for many people the nadir of building design, and it is not difficult to find examples of bland and cheap-looking architecture of that period. But others (led by the Twentieth Century Society) recognised the Civic Centre as embodying everything that civic planners of the age tried to achieve – angular shapes in white concrete and glass contrasting with groups of trees, ornamental paving and lawns.

In its listing record English Heritage describes it as "a particularly complete and coherent civic centre which compares well with others of its date ... In its careful massing and position it stands as a landmark within the city centre and embodies the hope and aspirations of a newly confident City Council following the devastation of the Second World War, and serves as a striking testimony to the spirit which guided the rebuilding of the city. Nowhere is this better reflected than in the Council House with its collection of artworks of rare quality and cohesion themed around Plymouth's history."

The Plan for Plymouth's post-war reconstruction included a new civic area which would enable all the council's offices to be brought under one roof. The award-winning overall design, clearly influenced by the United nations Building in New York, was by the City Architect, H J W Stirling, and construction started in 1957. The Civic Centre was opened by HM the Queen in 1962. It was not built on the cheap: the tower block is not the usual bland modernist box but has bowed ends with vertical glazed indents which echo the shape of the distinctive fly-away roof, and the quality of the detailing and internal decoration was high compared to other buildings of the period.

By the turn of the millennium, the City Council considered the building was no longer suitable for its needs. It needed work on the windows which were leaking, and the end panels required securing. Next to nothing had been spent on maintaining the building for many years. Many Plymothians supported its demolition, and were outraged when it was given a Grade II listing in 2007. The Council was forced to look for alternative uses for the building, and in 2015 the tower block was sold for redevelopment to the property developer Urban Splash. The Council retains the Chamber area.

We should beware the temptation to demolish buildings which no longer satisfy current tastes, and take care to retain the best of the past, whether it is fashionable or not. The Civic Centre may look to us like the components for a 1970s hi-fi system, but who knows what future generations will find appealing? The 1966 plan to do away with London's St Pancras Station Hotel, that flamboyant masterpiece of high Victorian Gothic, ought to serve as a lesson to us all.

20. THEATRE ROYAL BACKSTAGE TOURS

A behind-the-scenes look at the theatre

It was a bold move on the part of the City Council to construct a major theatre in Plymouth, for long known as a cultural backwater and 'garrison town'. But since Plymouth's Theatre Royal opened in 1982 it has never looked back. Plymouth has become a centre for new productions which later make their way to London's West End, and a venue for the main touring companies like Glyndebourne, Welsh Opera, the RSC, Matthew Bourne and Birmingham Royal Ballet, as well as innovative theatre and musicals. Its annual pantomime is among the nation's best. It is the largest and best attended regional producing theatre in the UK.

For this, much of the credit is due to the foresight and persistence of city councillors Tom Savery and Ralph Morrell in persuading the Council to go ahead with its construction, and to the artistic flair of Adrian Vinken, the Chief Executive since 1991.

With every theatrical production, so much more goes on behind the scenes than the audience might realise. The Theatre Royal organises backstage tours of the main theatre (the Lyric, one of the largest stages in the country) and the adjoining smaller venue (the Drum), including the orchestra pit, trap-rooms and front-of-house areas, and the Drum's highly flexible format, but also the dressing rooms, wings and backstage areas. Afternoon tea can be included in the ticket price.

The tours include steps and walkways on different levels and may not be suitable for everyone. Adapted tours can be organised for those with particular needs.

You can also have a tour around the theatre's production and learning centre (TR2) at Cattedown, where sets are constructed and costumes are put together, and where companies come to rehearse their productions. TR2 has won many international architectural awards, and was recognised as the UK's Building of the Year in 2003. It provides facilities which are unrivalled in the UK, and has strengthened Plymouth's reputation as the best place to put together new productions.

21. DERRY'S CLOCK AND THE BANK

Surviving nineteenth century buildings, the hub of pre-war Plymouth

Before the Second World War and the subsequent redesign of the city centre, this backwater, easily missed by the casual visitor, formed the heart of Plymouth. Derry's Clock stood at the junction of Union Street, George Street and Lockyer Street and nearby were the old Theatre Royal (a grand building in neo-classical style demolished in 1937 and replaced by what is now the defunct Reel Cinema), the offices of the London & South Western Railway Co, and the Wilts & Dorset Bank (incorporated into Lloyds Bank in 1914). Derry's Clock was the hub of the main tram routes from the city centre.

William Derry was the Mayor of Plymouth between 1861 and 1863, and again in 1879. In 1862 he presented the Town (as it then was) with a clock worth £220 together with half of the cost of the coloured limestone tower in which to display it. As the council did not have the necessary legal powers to construct a clock tower, it was officially a 'fountain', with three drinking fountains around the base. These remain, although it is not thought they were ever connected to a water supply.

The ornate Italianate bank, the 1930s cinema and Derry's Clock are the only buildings in the immediate vicinity to survive the Blitz and the post-war redevelopment, and both are Grade II listed. Despite rumours that the clock is not in its original position, both buildings stand where they have stood since the late nineteenth century, having weathered change and decay, the bombs and the demolition ball, and are an evocative reminder of just how much Plymouth has changed over the past century.

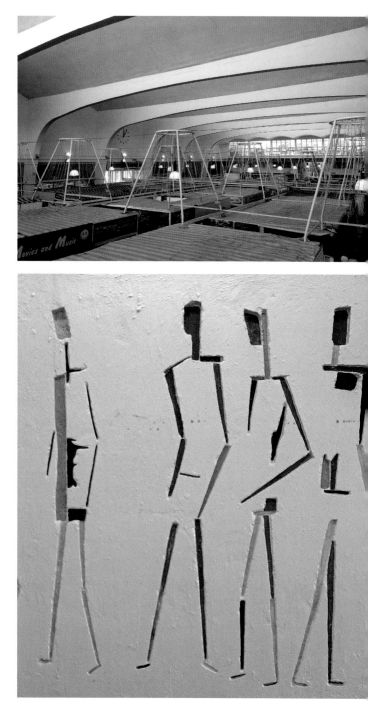

22. CITY MARKET, NEW GEORGE STREET

Innovative concrete design with period murals

As long ago as 1254, Sutton (the old manorial district which later became Plymouth) was granted the right to hold markets. In 1439 Parliament granted the town of Sutton Prior, the tithing of Sutton Raf and the hamlet of Sutton Valletort the status of the Borough of Plymouth, making Plymouth the first borough in the country to be established by Act of Parliament. The following year Henry VI granted a Royal Charter to the Mayor of Plymouth and Commonality for fairs, feasts and markets.

Following the redesign of the city centre in the 1950s, a new Pannier Market was built in the 'west end' between 1957 and 1959. It was the only major city centre structure to use local architects. The new market building used an innovative shell concrete system designed by the influential Polish engineer Albin Chronowicz, a former chief designer for British Reinforced Concrete. Shell concrete was pioneered in Germany before the war, but was only widely adopted in Britain afterwards, when shortages of steel and timber and rising costs made it an ideal solution for bridging large spans without using columns. It was Chronowicz' expertise in the use of shell concrete systems that allowed the architects, Walls & Pearn, to achieve such a big unsupported internal space, using vast, rippling roof spans which owe much to the Festival of Britain aesthetic.

In the north and south entrance halls are some typically 1950s murals by David Weeks, depicting shoppers and traders.

The shell-shaped sections of the roof with their north-facing roof-lights give a cool natural light across the interior. Beneath, there are over 140 different stalls selling everything from jewellery to geraniums, with craft stalls specialising in the sale or repair of specialist items. It has recently undergone a £3.5m make-over.

The Hoe

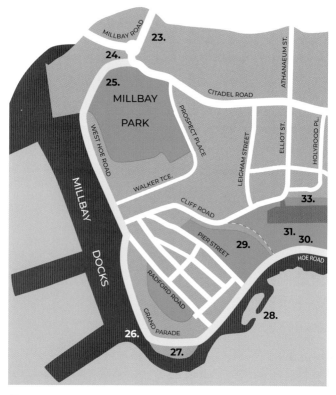

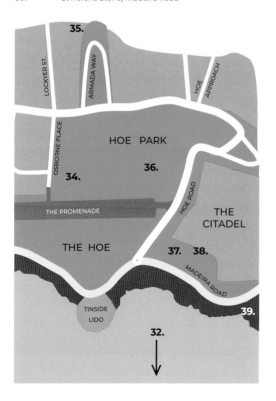

23. TEA AT THE TOP, DUKE OF CORNWALL HOTEL

Remarkable example of Victorian 'Domestic Gothic' style from the 1860s

When the South Devon Railway brought the broad gauge rails to Plymouth from Exeter in 1849, they built a terminus where Plymouth Pavilions now stands, known as Millbay Station. With regular trains to and from London, it was considered that a grand hotel close to the station was needed, and some of the directors of the railway company set about building one. The Duke of Cornwall Hotel was opened in 1865 immediately opposite the station entrance, and provided guests with amenities not previously available in Plymouth hotels, like hot and cold baths, billiard and smoking rooms, a ladies' drawing room and a French chef de cuisine.

The hotel's elaborately detailed Victorian Domestic Gothic styling survives more or less unaltered, complete with its cast-iron balconies and impossibly tall and narrow chimneys. Five different types of stone are used in the façade.

It survived the Second World War without damage despite its proximity to Millbay Docks, but was threatened with demolition in 1977. It was saved by local objectors, and not least by the support of Sir John Betjeman, who described it as one of the finest examples of Victorian gothic architecture he had ever seen. It has remained a popular choice for weddings, balls and special occasions.

The lighthouse-styled lantern – the tallest structure in Plymouth when it was built – is said to have been used to look out for incoming liners, so that porters could be despatched to Millbay before other hoteliers got wind of it. Couples can enjoy 'Tea at the Top' with their own butler, and panoramic views over Plymouth and the distant hills of Cornwall and Dartmoor. A champagne afternoon tea includes homemade scones, sandwiches and cakes (and a glass of champagne).

24. EDDYSTONE CIRCLE, WEST HOE ROAD

Why Smeaton's Tower was the first successful storm-proof lighthouse

The notorious Eddystone Reef, 14 miles south of Plymouth Sound, was a major hazard for ships, as it rises only a few feet above the waves at high tide and at night could only be avoided by meticulous navigation. Given the difficulty of gaining a foothold on the rocks in the steep swell of the Channel, it was an awkward place to build a lighthouse. The first attempt to place a light was a somewhat flamboyant wooden structure erected in 1698 by Henry Winstanley, but this was washed away in a storm only five years later, taking its designer with it. A second lighthouse using stone and timber was built by John Rudyerd in 1711 which was more successful, but that was destroyed by fire (always a hazard with candle-power) in 1755.

John Smeaton was a talented engineer who is regarded as the 'father of civil engineering'. He made his name by developing a type of mortar capable of setting underwater, thereby pioneering Portland cement and indeed the use of concrete as a modern building material. He was engaged by Trinity House to design a third lighthouse.

Smeaton's lighthouse consisted entirely of stone, and work was begun in 1756, being completed only three years later. The tower is shaped like an oak tree, with a wide base, and made with granite blocks weighing about a ton, cut so as to dovetail with adjoining blocks as shown in the pavement feature opposite the Duke of Cornwall Hotel. Each layer of blocks was anchored to the layer above by oak key wedges, represented by the small square pieces. The pavement feature is not of course to scale, as the actual structure is much bigger, but it helps us understand why the lighthouse is so important historically.

On 16 October 1759 the 24 candles used for the light were lit for the first time (they were replaced by oil lamps and reflectors in 1810). The lighthouse proved entirely successful and withstood the strongest storms, such as that of 1804 when four naval ships were wrecked while at anchor in the Cattewater, and the one of 1817 which washed away part of Breakwater which was then under construction. Unfortunately, over time the rock on which it stood became undermined by the sea, and by the 1870s the lighthouse men had to endure alarming swaying and shuddering movements during major storms.

A new lighthouse was built alongside, designed by James Douglass, using Smeaton's design principles as improved by Robert Stevenson (the engineer responsible for the Bell Rock Lighthouse). This first shone in 1882 and remains in use. The plan was to demolish Smeaton's lighthouse, but civil engineers held Smeaton in such regard that money was raised to dismantle it and re-erect it on Plymouth Hoe. The foundations and lower section remain on the Eddystone Rock alongside the new light, proving too difficult to dislodge.

Smeaton's Tower (as it is known) was depicted on the old penny coin behind the figure of Britannia seated on her rocky throne, from 1860 to 1894 and again from 1937 until decimalisation of the coinage in 1971.

25. FORMER MILL PRISON, WEST HOE ROAD

Where French and American prisoners of war were incarcerated

Next to the Duke of Cornwall Hotel is a small park, planted with trees and backed by a military security fence. This is the site of the Mill Prison, in which hundreds of French and American prisoners of war were kept during the American War of Independence of 1775 to 1783, the wars against France between 1793 and 1815, and the Anglo-American War of 1812 to 1815.

We know something of the prison from a report in 1784 by the Quaker John Howard, a committed prison reformer who has given his name to the Howard League for Prison Reform. Howard records that there were 392 French and 298 American prisoners of war at Mill Prison in 1779, as well as some 400 or more on a prison hulk moored in the Hamoaze. Between 1777 and 1783 a total of 10,352 prisoners of war passed through Plymouth (most of them French), of whom 179 died, and one (no doubt to the great surprise of the guards) gave birth to a child.

By 1801 Mill Prison was full, and there was a growing fear of a prison uprising or mass break-out which would have had calamitous consequences for the naval establishment at Plymouth Dock. It was decided to build a prison on moorland to the north of Plymouth where the risk of escape would be much reduced, and accordingly Dartmoor Prison was constructed between 1806 and 1809. From 1813 until 1815 about 6,500 American sailors were imprisoned at Dartmoor. The prisoners were permitted to be largely self-governing, with their own 'courts', market, theatre and even a gambling room. Indeed, as Howard noted in his report on the Mill Prison, the Americans tended to be treated rather better than the French, with better accommodation and better food.

Some prisoners would relieve their boredom and make some money by carving elaborate ships and other objects from bone. Examples of these can be seen at The Box, Plymouth's new museum.

26. OLD CUSTOMS HOUSE, MILLBAY DOCKS

Adjoining Millbay Pier where liner passengers came ashore

Millbay Docks is a mere shadow of what it once was: a few derelict piers and acres of wasteland or tarmac where once there were busy warehouses and an inner harbour with a graving dock. The only thriving part is the roll-on, roll-off ferry operated by Brittany Ferries. The area is now earmarked for an ambitious urban regeneration programme.

Until the mid-1700s Millbay was a muddy inlet backed by an area of marshland known as the Sourpool, where Union Street now runs. In 1756 John Smeaton dredged a channel and built a jetty where masonry for the Eddystone lighthouse was loaded, but the development of the docks started in 1844 when Millbay Pier (seen beyond the customs house) was built to serve the limestone quarries at West Hoe. I K Brunel's great ship, the SS *Great Britain*, berthed here during her maiden voyage to New York in 1845 and was visited by 15,000 sightseers. The owner of the quarries and pier, Thomas Gill, was also chairman of the South Devon Railway. By the time the railway reached Plymouth in 1849, the Great Western Dock Co had been formed, with Brunel as engineer, and the line was extended from its terminus at Millbay Station down to the docks. Customs facilities were granted for Millbay Pier, and the graceful octagonal Customs House was built.

For the next 100 years or so, the docks were a major commercial port, handling imported grain and timber and a wide variety of freight. Willoughby Bros built ships in the graving dock, as well as chain ferries for Torpoint and Saltash. In the days of ocean liners it was quicker and more convenient for passengers from America to be brought ashore at Plymouth and take the Great Western's Ocean Mail expresses to London, than for the ship to sail on up the Channel to Southampton or London. The Ocean Mail carriages were drawn up adjacent to Millbay Pier where the passengers would disembark from the GWR's paddle-tenders, and the train would then be hauled to Millbay Station. From there the Ocean Mail travelled non-stop to London Paddington.

By the 1930s some 700 liners a year made a stop at Plymouth, including the RMS *Queen Mary* and other Cunarders, and as many as 38,000 passengers disembarked. Most came ashore here at Millbay Pier and travelled on to London. Famous visitors included Charlie Chaplin, Laurel and Hardy, and 167 of the surviving crew members of RMS *Titanic*, who entered Plymouth Sound in April 1912 aboard the Lapland. They were transferred to one of the GWR tenders to be brought ashore at Millbay, but instead of landing they were kept on board until each had been served with a summons requiring them to give evidence to the Receiver of Wrecks. They were then prevented from leaving the docks (presumably until they had each made a formal statement), but were so incensed by their treatment that they refused to give any evidence at all until their illegal detention was lifted. They must have thought this a poor welcome indeed after the nightmare they had endured.

27. RUSTY ANCHOR PASSAGE, GRAND PARADE

Ship models, and Plymouth's Waterfront Walkway

This passage around the front of an imposing nineteenth century terrace is known as Rusty Anchor, although no anchor – rusty or otherwise – is now evident. Instead there are several of these models of naval ships. Rusty Anchor has always been a favourite place from which to see large naval vessels as they enter or leave Devonport, since the deep-water channel runs close to the shore.

Devonport is the largest naval base in Western Europe. Ship movements have become more frequent in recent years, since Devonport became a venue for fleet operational sea training (variously known by the acronyms of FOST and BOST, for basic operational sea training). As well as training Royal Navy personnel, it is an important source of revenue in training foreign naval crews to handle their vessels in battle. FOST certifies crews and vessels as being sufficiently prepared for any eventuality through rigorous exercises and readiness inspections. When the USS *Forrest Sherman* underwent a short version of BOST in 2012, one sailor commented "I've been through other exercises, inspections and deployment and this was by far the hardest ... more intense than INSURV". Dutch, Spanish and German vessels.

These ship models are just part of an impressive series of plaques and sculptures placed along the route of the South West Coast Path between Admiral's Hard, Stonehouse, where the foot ferry lands walkers from Cornwall, and Jennycliff on the east side of the Sound, where Plymouth's boundary is marked by a 'welcome mat'. Many of them feature in this guide. A well-illustrated brochure showing points of interest along the route can be obtained free from the Tourist Information Centre or Plymouth City Council.

28. WEST HOE PIER, HOE ROAD

Where Sir Francis Chichester landed after his epic circumnavigation

This little harbour is where Francis Chichester stepped ashore on the 28th May 1967 after completing his solo round-the-world voyage, having sailed 28,500 miles in just 274 days (226 days' actual sailing time) and with only one stop. The building that is now the Waterfront Restaurant was then the club house of the Royal Western Yacht Club, and the point where the Fastnet and other oceanic races started.

Sir Francis Chichester (he was knighted by the Queen after the voyage) was one of those larger-than-life characters of whom Britain has produced more than its fair share. Born in 1901 in a rectory near Barnstaple in North Devon, he emigrated to New Zealand when he was 18 and in ten years built up a prosperous forestry and mining business, only to suffer severe losses in the Great Depression of 1929.

He returned to England and learned to fly, acquiring a de Havilland Gypsy Moth open cockpit biplane in which he flew to New Zealand. His attempt to set a new record failed due to engine problems, although he completed the flight, using an ingenious method of navigation which enabled him to plot his position accurately on a knee-board while flying the plane.

Having completed this and other flights he planned to make a solo circumnavigation by air, but unfortunately he collided with a power line in Japan and sustained serious injuries. Too old to join the RAF during the Second World War, he became an air navigation instructor.

In 1958, at the age of 57, he was diagnosed with terminal lung cancer, and he adopted a strict diet. With his cancer in remission, he took up long-distance yachting, and after only a year won the first single-handed trans-Atlantic race in 1960 in *Gypsy Moth III*.

He was 64 years old when he set off from here on 27 August 1966 in the *Gypsy Moth IV* to attempt the first non-stop solo circumnavigation. The wooden boat (built to his own specification) was 56ft long and – as he admitted on his return – much too big for him. "She is cantankerous and difficult and needs a crew of three: a man to navigate, an elephant to move the tiller and chimpanzee with arms eight feet long to get about below and work some of the gear". He had problems with the self-steering gear and the boat's tendency to veer to windward, which continued despite some repairs at his only stop in Sydney. The voyage took him past the notorious Cape Horn, where he encountered tremendous waves "like great sloping walls" towering behind him, some of them 50ft high, which filled the cockpit five times.

It was a remarkable achievement by any standards, and on his return to Plymouth he was met by hundreds of boats, thousands of cheering spectators, a ten-gun salute from the Royal Citadel, and the attention of the world's press.

29. WEST HOE PARK

Former quarry, now a park and children's play area

The grey Plymouth limestone is everywhere in Plymouth: in the walls of the Citadel, the stern Victorian school buildings, the Guildhall, St Andrew's Minster and the Royal William Yard. It is comparatively easy to quarry, and there are abundant and accessible supplies of rock from the Hoe eastwards alongside the Plym estuary at the Cattewater. Quarrying became a major industry in the nineteenth century, and vast quantities were obtained to supply the needs of Plymouth Breakwater. Such was the demand for Plymouth Rock that Mountbatten would have been quarried away had it not been for a public outcry.

The quarry at West Hoe was owned by Thomas Gill, who was one of Plymouth's chief entrepreneurs of the Industrial Revolution. He built the soap factory at Millbay in 1818 and, as we have seen, was one of the directors of the South Devon Railway and built the pier at the entrance to Mill Bay. He later became mayor and Liberal MP for Plymouth. Limestone from his quarry was burnt in limekilns for fertiliser as well as being sold for building stone. In order to improve the access to wharves where the stone could be loaded onto barges, he constructed the basin at West Hoe Pier and linked it to his quarry by a light railway which passed through a tunnel beneath Hoe Road. Quarrying here was a lucrative business, as the level quarry floor could be sold for building land, and West Hoe was extensively developed after the quarry closed in 1875, with grand terraces facing the sea and smaller ones behind.

Part of West Hoe Quarry is now a pleasant park, backed by the cliff left after quarrying ceased. There are fissures and caves in the rock face where fossils have been found. The park is popular with small children, having a pirate-themed play area, a circular train ride from which the "ding, ding" of little hands on bells never seems to cease, crazy golf, and climbing frames concealed among the leafy pathways.

30. THE BELVEDERE, HOE ROAD

Old bull-baiting ring which faced Plymouth's 'banjo' pier

The colonnaded Belvedere, descending in tiers from the Hoe down to Madeira Road like a wedding cake, seems to us now a rather pointless affair, the sort of place where Victorian and Edwardian ladies would sit decorously to admire the view while Pater took the children down to the rocks to paddle and catch crabs. But it was built to face not just the Sound, but Plymouth's Pier, where there would always have been something to look at, something going on.

The banjo-shaped Pier was opened in 1884, originally with just a windscreen around a bandstand at the business end, but this was roofed over in 1891 to form a 2,000 seat concert hall. As well as band concerts, this was used for roller-skating, dancing, boxing and wrestling. Local lads used the pier for fishing and diving, and there were boat excursions around the Sound from its landing stage. Unfortunately it never proved a success. Perhaps the Plymouth weather deterred the crowds, but its struggle to remain solvent ended with the appointment of receivers in 1938. It was severely damaged by incendiary bombs in 1941 and the charred remains were removed in 1953.

The flattened area immediately in front of the Belvedere known as the Bull Ring was indeed originally a ring or pit for bull-baiting. This was a cruel sport which was popular from about the thirteenth to the early nineteenth century, where a bull would be tethered to a stake and dogs trained for the task would attack it, usually by fastening its jaws to the bull's snout. The bull would try to defend itself by throwing the dog into the air with a toss of its head, or impale it on its horns. Bulldogs were specially bred for the task, as were Pit Bull terriers, and were chosen for their courage, power and ferocity.

The Bull Ring has several small memorials including one that lists the names of all the maritime personnel who died in the Falklands War of 1982, and the vessels from the Royal Navy, Royal Fleet Auxiliary and the Merchant Navy which took part.

31. THE BEATLES' BUMS, THE HOE

Recalling the Fab Four's visit to Plymouth in 1967

1967: the supertanker Torrey Canyon struck the Seven Stones reef off Land's End, spilling its cargo of crude oil along the Cornish coast; Jimi Hendrix set fire to his guitar on stage and had to be taken to hospital to treat the burns to his hands; Prime Minister Harold Wilson announced that Britain would be joining the European Economic Community (as it then was); the *QE2* was launched; and Sergeant Pepper's Lonely Hearts Club Band was released by the Beatles.

That year, the Beatles also made a visit to Plymouth. In 1963 and 1964 they had played to a full house at the ABC Theatre (later the Reel cinema) at Derry's Cross, supported by now-forgotten bands like The Kestrels, Peter Jay and the Jaywalkers, and the Remo Four. Those who were there recall that they could hear virtually nothing of the music because all the girls were screaming.

What brought the Beatles to relax on Plymouth Hoe was a mishap during the filming of A Magical Mystery Tour, when the coach featured in the film got wedged between the parapets of a narrow bridge near Poundsgate, on Dartmoor. Tempers frayed and the group decided to take a break in Plymouth, lunching at the Grand Hotel and doing a publicity photograph on the Hoe. The photograph shown on the display board was taken by their photographer, David Redfern, and their clothes are those they wore in the film.

The places where John, Paul, George and Ringo sat on the grass overlooking Plymouth Sound have been lovingly marked with these copper plaques set into the grass, enabling anyone to sit where those famous bums once sat, half a century ago.

32. THE BREAKWATER

The world's first successful deep–water wave breaker

Seen from Plymouth Hoe, the Breakwater is just a thin line across the mouth of the Sound, looking rather like a giant submarine with the Breakwater Fort as a conning tower. But like an iceberg, most of it lies beneath the waves. It is one of the engineering marvels of the early nineteenth century.

Plymouth Sound and the estuaries of the River Tamar and River Plym together give Plymouth one of the world's finest natural harbours, and the largest naval base in Western Europe. But the Sound was open to storms from the south and south-west, and warships at anchor were vulnerable. In 1804 (the year before the Battle of Trafalgar) ten ships at anchor in the Cattewater were wrecked in a single day, with waves surging over the neck of land between Mount Batten and Dunstone Point. Lord Howe, the Admiral of the Fleet, complained that Plymouth Sound would be the "graveyard of the British Fleet".

In 1806 the Admiralty commissioned a report from John Rennie, a civil engineer responsible for many major engineering projects, and Joseph Whidbey, a marine surveyor who had sailed with George Vancouver during his voyage of exploration to Puget Sound in 1792, as to the best way to improve the safety of vessels moored in the Sound. They proposed a free-standing breakwater nearly a mile long, constructed on a convenient shoal in the middle of the Sound. The cost was estimated at about £1,170,000. As a proportion of the country's total output or GDP, this represents over £6 billion in today's money, and it is hardly surprising it took until 1811 for the government to approve the project. The Plymouth Breakwater was heralded as the greatest public work undertaken in the country since the building of Hadrian's Wall, and was comparable with the construction of the Channel Tunnel in our own day.

Quarrying the immense amount of rock needed for the task began in 1812, with limestone hewn from the cliffs either side of the Cattewater. This was loaded onto barges and dropped onto the sea bed to form an artificial shoal. Work progressed fast, and already by 1815 (the year of the Battle of Waterloo) much of the shoal was visible above the surface. A hurricane in January 1817 shifted some of the rock which had been laid, but the general opinion was that but for the Breakwater, all the ships at anchor in the Cattewater would have been wrecked and many of the buildings on the shore swept away.

Another violent storm in November 1824 displaced more than 200,000 tons of rock and altered the seaward slope. This time, rather than drag it back into place, it was decided to work with nature rather than struggle against her, and nature's slope was retained. The design was adapted with a smooth surface on the seaward side so as to form an artificial reef rather than a sea wall. During storms the Breakwater is often invisible beneath the swirl of white water, but it still stands firm, continuing to protect the Sound some 170 years after it was completed in the 1840s. Ultimately some 4½ million tons of rock were laid, and huge concrete blocks continue to be added to the seaward side to help break the power of the Atlantic waves.

33. ASTOR HOUSE, ELLIOT TERRACE

The home of Nancy Astor, the first woman MP to sit in Parliament

Elliot Terrace is an ornate Italianate terrace facing the Hoe, built in 1860. No.3, the home of Lord and Lady Astor, was bequeathed to Plymouth City Council, and can be visited by prior arrangement.

Nancy Astor was the first woman to sit as a Member of Parliament. She was born in 1879 in Virginia, the seventh child of a railroad entrepreneur, and was a noted beauty. Following a disastrous first marriage, she moved to England and fell in love with the country and with Waldorf Astor, whose father had inherited a personal fortune that made him the richest man in America, and who had taken British citizenship in 1899. They married in 1906. Nancy later quipped, "I married beneath me – all women do", although this was hardly fair to Waldorf, who became a prominent politician and philanthropist.

Nancy became a socialite and society hostess. She was a feisty woman and never at a loss for words, and though liberal in some respects she disliked Jews and Catholics, and was a strong advocate of Christian Science and teetotalism. When Waldorf became Viscount Astor on the death of his father in 1919 and gave up his seat as MP for Plymouth Sutton, she decided she would stand in his place. Despite her ignorance of current political issues, her ready wit and informality appealed to voters. She could always turn the tables on hecklers, but she must have been at a loss for words on one occasion, while canvassing in Plymouth with a naval officer to accompany her. At one house she was greeted by a girl who said: "Mum's out, but she said if a lady comes with a sailor they're to use the upstairs room and leave ten bob".

She won the election and took her seat in December 1919 as the first woman to sit in Parliament. She never held a position with much influence or any ministerial post, although she did succeed in getting an Act passed prohibiting young people under 18 from drinking alcohol without parental approval, and supported the socialist Margaret McMillan in developing nursery schools.

As the 1930s wore on, she seemed to become out of touch politically. She criticised the Nazis for their dismissive attitude towards women, and on meeting Ribbentrop, the German ambassador, she remarked that Hitler would never be taken seriously in England because he looked too much like Charlie Chaplin. But she supported appeasement, and approved of Hitler's opposition to Communists and Jews.

Despite her opposition to the war, Lady Astor will always be remembered for leading the dancing on the Hoe during the darkest days of the Blitz, and for her impulsive generosity towards those in need. She and Waldorf served the city as Lord Mayor and Lady Mayoress from 1939-44. In 1945 she stood down as MP, disillusioned and politically isolated. She died in 1964.

34. THE HOE BOWLING GREEN

Sir Francis Drake and the news of the Spanish Armada

Everyone knows about Sir Francis Drake: the keen yachtsman (famously circumcising the globe with his great cutter, the *Golden Hinde*), explorer (discovering the island which bears his name), sportsman (a noted slow bowler, playing for the Devon Dumplings), hairdresser (singeing the King of Spain's beard, a method of restricting beard growth), and musician (drummer with the Full Fathom Five, with his own drum kit which can still be seen at Buckland Abbey). In his spare time he indulged in a spot of piracy.

Not really. But he was certainly a larger-than-life figure both in life and in history, who left his mark on the city and is its greatest hero. Drake was born at Crowndale Farm near Tavistock, the eldest of 12 sons. Fearing attack during the Prayer Book Rebellion by the Cornish in 1549, the family fled to Kent. Drake later returned to Plymouth and took up with his cousin John Hawkins, who he accompanied on several of his voyages. Like Hawkins, Drake became a privateer, plundering Spanish treasure ships on the Queen's behalf.

In May 1588 the most powerful fleet the world had seen left Corunna, bound for England, with 130 ships, 8,000 sailors and 18,000 soldiers. It took two days just to leave port. This was the *Grande y Felicíssima Armada* sent by the fanatically Catholic King Philip II of Spain to take Protestant England and depose Queen Elizabeth. The English fleet, consisting of the 34 ships of the Royal Fleet and 163 other ships (including 12 privateers) under the command of Lord Howard of Effingham, had been hastily assembled at Plymouth, watching for the blaze of the beacon on Penlee Point warning of the Armada's approach. The English ships were smaller and more lightly armed, but thanks to the improvements in ship design introduced by John Hawkins as Comptroller of the Navy, they were faster and more manoeuvrable than the towering Spanish galleons.

Drake, the Vice Admiral, was playing bowls on Plymouth Hoe when the news reached Plymouth on 29 July 1588 that the Spanish Armada had been sighted off the Cornish coast. "Time enough to play the game and thrash the Spaniards afterwards", he is said to have told the messenger. With the tide flooding into Plymouth Sound and a stiff south-west breeze blowing, he would have known that there was plenty of time to finish his game before the tide turned so that the fleet could sail.

Not that those were his actual words, of course. He was a Tavistock man, the son of a farmer, and like Devonians everywhere he didn't like to be rushed. What he actually said was: "Yer, stiddy on, young man! Us can only do wan thing to a time. Us'll vinish this-yer game of bowls, an' then us'll go an' say 'owdy-do' to they Spanish gen'l'men in the proper manner. Now ... 'tis your go, Jethro." Oh yes he did.

Although the Hoe Bowling Green is not where Francis Drake played, it reminds us of the best-known incident in the life of this remarkable man.

35. CHURCH OF CHRIST THE KING, NOTTE STREET

Sir Giles Gilbert Scott's last work

Sir Giles Gilbert Scott (1880-1960) was one of the most accomplished architects of the twentieth century, responsible for Liverpool's massive Anglican Cathedral, the Bankside Power Station (now the Tate Modern), Battersea Power Station (now a major development site incorporating the famous 'upturned table legs'), and the once ubiquitous red GPO telephone kiosk. He was the grandson of the equally celebrated Sir George Gilbert Scott, the master of high Victorian Gothic architecture, who amongst other things designed the Albert Memorial and St Pancras Station Hotel.

Giles Scott was adept at blending Gothic styling with contemporary, and this is nowhere more evident than in his last work, the Roman Catholic Church of Christ the King in Armada Way, at the lower (northern) side of Hoe Park. Scott was working on the design when he was admitted to hospital with terminal cancer in 1960. He took the designs with him into hospital and continued to revise them until his death aged 79. The church was built posthumously in 1961-62.

It was paid for by an anonymous donor who stipulated a conservative design, and is thus highly characteristic of Scott's own approach. The presbytery and hall on the Hoe side of the church were designed by Scott's son, Richard Gilbert Scott, and added later.

The church served originally as a 'chapel-of-ease' for the Roman Catholic Cathedral in Wyndham Street, but in 1988 it became the Catholic Chaplaincy for Plymouth's growing student population.

36. EXECUTION MARK, THE HOE

The site of Plymouth's last public execution in 1797

The French Revolution of 1789 to 1795 and the execution of the French king Louis XVI sent shivers of horror through the British establishment. Radical groups, encouraged by developments in France and by the publication of Paine's The Rights of Man, actively plotted the revolutionary overthrow of the monarchy and the government. In 1797 the British Navy mutinied at Spithead and the Nore, chiefly because of the appalling conditions under which sailors had to serve, with low pay, harsh punishments, and the ever-present risk of serious injury or death for which no compensation was paid. Later that year the crew of HMS *Hermione* mutinied in the West Indies, killing most of the officers in revenge for an incident in which the bodies of three men, who had fallen from the rigging in a desperate scramble to avoid a flogging for being the last man down on deck, were unceremoniously thrown overboard.

The mutiny spread to Plymouth, where sailors went on strike and evicted officers from their ships. Officers who had ill-treated them were paraded through the streets and imprisoned in the lock-up at Plymouth Dock. The Naval authorities responded decisively and harshly, with the ringleaders hanged from the yard-arm or transported to Botany Bay.

In July 1797 three Royal Marines were found guilty of attempting to incite a mutiny at Stonehouse Barracks and were sentenced to death by firing squad. On 8 July all troops serving in Plymouth were marched to the Hoe and formed up in a semi-circle to witness the execution. At 1.30pm the three men, Lee, Coffy and Branning, were marched from the west gate of the Citadel preceded by the Royal Marine band playing the Dead March from Handel's oratorio Saul. They were given the last rites by members of the clergy before being made to kneel on their coffins. Then (according to one newspaper account) "an officer of marines came and drew the caps over their faces, and a party of twenty marines immediately came down and put a period to their existence by discharging the contents of their muskets through their bodies".

This was not the whole story. Coffy and Branning were killed by the first volley, but Lee was not. A reserve squad was then brought in to carry out the sentence, but they also missed (one assumes, deliberately). The sergeant responsible for the firing party then despatched him at close quarters with a shot to the head.

"After which all the regiments marched round them in solemn procession, the whole forming, perhaps, one of the most awful scenes that the human eye ever witnessed". It was said that about 30,000 people were present, including much of the Fleet and many of the local inhabitants.

It is sometimes said that this mark – a cross with a number 3 in the centre – does not commemorate Plymouth's last public execution, but is one of the boundary markers for the edge of the glacis surrounding the Citadel. There is however such a boundary mark at the top of Castle Street, and the difference between them suggests that this is indeed a commemorative mark.

37. THE LEGEND OF GOGMAGOG, THE HOE

Giants and Trojans, Gogmagog, Brutus and Corineus

Had you been able to sail into Plymouth Sound prior to about 1660, the most prominent man-made feature you would have noticed would be two giant figures carved into the turf of the slope below the Hoe, their outlines delineated by the lighter-coloured rock beneath. They may have been seen by Roman traders from Bordeaux when they came to Hooe for cargoes of tin, cattle and hides, by Breton raiders as they came to plunder the settlement at Sutton Pool, and by the Pilgrims as they left Plymouth for the New World. Unfortunately no one knows when the figures were first made.

The legend surrounding Gog and Magog appears to have started with the twelfth century cleric, Geoffrey of Monmouth (never a reliable historian), in his largely fictional *History of the Kings of Britain*. Following the sack of Troy in 1184 BC, so the story goes, a group of Trojans led by Brutus and Corineus sailed from the eastern Mediterranean to Britain, landing at Plymouth (or Totnes, or somewhere - accounts differ). The country was then occupied by a race of giants, but the Trojans saw them off and took it over, naming it Britain after Brutus. The land west of the Tamar was given to Corineus, after whom Cornwall was named.

There are different versions of the legend, but one has it that the Trojans/Britons were having a festival on the Hoe to celebrate their victory, when they were attacked by some of the giants. Annoyed at their impertinence in gate-crashing the party, the Trojans slaughtered them all apart from Gogmagog, a 20ft giant, who was wrestled by Corineus and thrown over the cliffs into the sea, where his blood stained the cliffs red. The figures of Gogmagog and Corineus were said to be carved into the turf to commemorate this feat.

Sutton Pool and the area around Hooe Lake were continuously occupied from the Bronze Age (around 2,000 BC to 500 BC) to the present. Iron Age finds have been made at Mount Batten and Hooe Lake, including coins, pottery, mirrors, and a burial ground. The practice of carving giant figures into hillsides – typically horses or men with clubs – dates from the Iron Age (around 500 BC to 100 AD).

However, it has also been suggested that the figures were carved to celebrate the Act of Incorporation of the Borough of Plymouth in 1439, as the first known reference to them was in 1495.

Richard Carew in his Survey of Cornwall of 1602 describes the figures as two men, one bigger than the other, with clubs in their hands. Other accounts say that the smaller figure had no club and may have been female. Sadly no representation of the two figures has survived, and their precise location is unknown. The figures disappeared when the Citadel was constructed in the 1660s. They were re-imagined by artist Charles Newington (who was responsible for the White Horse at Folkestone) and installed on a temporary basis in June 2021. The project was sponsored by the Plymouth Waterfront Partnership.

38. ROYAL MARINES MEMORIAL, THE HOE

The unseen war memorial

The Hoe is dominated by the great Naval Monument, erected by the Admiralty in 1924 to commemorate those who died at sea and have no known grave. It was expanded after the Second World War, and now bears the names of 7,251 sailors of Britain and the Commonwealth who died in the First World War and 15,933 who died in the Second. There are similar monuments at Portsmouth and Chatham. The monument stands at the south end of Armada Way, which runs from here across the City Centre to North Cross.

Near it is a rather modest monument erected in 1989 to the 107,000 members of the Royal Air Force who died between 1939 and 1945. This is the only known monument to the allied air forces. There is also a recently-erected monument honouring those in the Merchant Navy and fishing fleet who have been lost at sea in times of peace and war. More than 30,000 merchant seamen and trawlermen lost their lives during the Second World War, a death rate that was proportionately higher than that of any of the armed forces.

Some distance away from the Naval and RAF monuments, beneath the walls of the Citadel, stands this fine memorial to the Royal Marines, erected in 1921. Its position, at some distance from the other memorials and separated from them by a sunken road, somehow makes this one all the more poignant. The granite pedestal is surmounted by a bronze figure of Saint George, who appears to be doing something nasty with a dagger to a mythical beast. The wing which appears to belong to St George is one of the beast's wings, and the other one is shown broken at his feet. One account of the sculpture describes the beast as representing 'militarism', no doubt in reference to Germany, and its brutal annexation of Belgium which precipitated Britain's declaration of war and the conflict in which so many died.

The tablet has a quotation from Pilgrim's Progress: "So he passed over and all the trumpets sounded for him on the other side".

Beside the pedestal are two stone figures. The one on the left is *Per Mare* (by sea) and shows a Royal Marine in shirt and trousers, holding a ram-rod. The one on the right, *Per Terram* (by land), is a Marine in fighting order, wearing a greatcoat and tin helmet, with his weapon reversed in mourning for his lost colleagues.

Strangely, there is no Army memorial on the Hoe, although there are many Remembrance crosses throughout the city giving the names of people in the locality who died in war. There is however a monument to the officers and men of the Devon, Somerset and Gloucester Regiments who fell in the Boer War between 1899 and 1902, which stands opposite the north-west corner of the Citadel. Beneath an obelisk are bronze bas-reliefs listing key battles, and commemorating one of Queen Victoria's grandsons, Prince Christian Victor, who died of malaria in Pretoria in 1900. Opposite the entrance to the Citadel there is also a 2011 memorial to all the soldiers of 29 Commando killed in action since 1962.

39. ST HELENA STONE, MADEIRA ROAD

Recalling Napoleon's visit to Plymouth in 1815

On 26 July 1815 a visitor arrived in Plymouth Sound who caused more than a little excitement: the former French Emperor Napoleon, who was a 'guest of His Majesty' aboard HMS *Bellerophon* following his defeat at the Battle of Waterloo and his subsequent abdication. He had been prevented from escaping to the USA by the British naval blockade of French ports, and had surrendered to Captain Maitland of the *Bellerophon*. Captain Maitland initially anchored in Torbay, but was ordered to proceed to the more sheltered anchorage of Plymouth Sound while the government decided what to do with 'General Bonaparte'. Contemporary paintings show the *Bellerophon* anchored off Staddon Heights on the east side of the Sound, with two frigates moored nearby.

Everyone wanted to catch a glimpse of Napoleon, this man who inspired admiration and fear in equal measure, who had blazed a trail of conquest throughout Europe and as far as Egypt and the gates of Moscow. Despite an order that all boats were to keep a cable's length (200 yds) from the *Bellerophon*, boats crowded round the ship with visitors from all over the Westcountry and further afield. At one point Captain Maitland estimated there were around 1,000 boats filled with sightseers desperate for a glimpse of the great man. The painting opposite, by Jules Girardet, was made some years after the event, but well illustrates the extraordinary fascination which Napoleon inspired. A gravestone in the churchyard of Stoke Damerel records the death of a stonemason in the Dockyard "who was unfortunately Drowned between the Island and Point Returning from seeing BONAPARTE in the Sound".

Napoleon was treated with considerable deference by the officers of the *Bellerophon*, and a correspondent in *The Times* complained that they kept their heads uncovered while he was on deck, as if he were royalty. Napoleon, of course, had no doubt that he was royalty, and he graciously condescended to appear at the ship's side every evening at about 6pm for several minutes, so that the public's interest in him might be satisfied.

It seems that Napoleon expected that he would be allowed to settle in England, and perhaps granted a country estate. On being informed that his fate would be custodial exile on the remote South Atlantic island of St Helena, he wrote: "I appeal to History; it will say that an enemy, who for twenty years waged war against the English people, came voluntarily, in his misfortunes, to seek asylum under their laws. What more brilliant proof could he give of his esteem and confidence? But what return did England make for such magnanimity?"

It is difficult to see what actions of his justified any magnanimity on England's part. After all, on the previous occasion when he had abdicated (after the disastrous retreat from Moscow) he had been exiled to Elba, but nevertheless returned to France and resumed his imperial throne for 100 days until the bloodiest battle of them all finally ended his ambitions. This piece of rock from St Helena, put in place 200 years later, reminds us of his brief visit.

PLACES CALLED PLYMOUTH

In 1621 the Pilgrim Fathers and their families shared a meal with members of the indigenous Pokanoket tribe in a place they named Plymouth, after the town from which they had departed the shores of England. This Plymouth, in what is now the State of Massachusetts, is the first and best-known Plymouth in the USA. It is among the state's larger cities with a population of 57,000. A reconstruction of the settlement as it might have looked in the seventeenth century is a popular tourist attraction.

Plymouth, Minnesota, is the largest municipality with the same name in the United States. Its population is about 74,000. The smallest Plymouth is a township of 46 residents in North Dakota. In contrast, the population of Plymouth, England is about 265,000.

In Wisconsin there are three Plymouths. In Ohio there are also three, and there are two in Michigan. Figures on websites for the total number of Plymouths in the USA vary from 20 to 34 - the discrepancy may be due to double-counting, where a city has more than one postal entry. There appear to be 26 in total.

Elsewhere in the world, there are two Plymouths in Nova Scotia, and one each in New Zealand, Tobago, Haiti and Montserrat.

As for the total number of Plymouths or New Plymouths in the world, estimates vary from 31 to 51. There are even two Plymouths in Wales (both electoral wards, one in Merthyr Tydfil and one in Penarth). In all, there are at least 40 Plymouths around the world, not counting the old original standing at the mouth of the River Plym.

PLYMOUTH'S EARLIEST, OLDEST, BIGGEST

Plymouth boasts the first successful sea-based lighthouse, the first successful deep water breakwater, the first hospital built on hygienic principles, the first successful porcelain manufactured outside China, the first 6 inch Ordnance Survey map, the first stamp collector, and the first self-service petrol filling station - and is where Farley's Rusks, the Trunki ride-on suitcase and the Walker wing-sail were developed.

It has the country's oldest gin distillery, the oldest commercial bakery, the oldest covered naval slipway, the oldest Ashkenazi synagogue, the most cobbled streets, the deepest shark tank and the most advanced wave tank, the world's largest unmanned underwater vehicle, the most number of listed post-war buildings outside London, the youngest listed building, the world's longest-running marine science survey, and Europe's biggest naval base. Plymouth Sound is the oldest continually studied marine area in the world.

PLYMOUTH PEOPLE

A selection of notable people born in or associated with Plymouth:

Explorers

Sir Francis Drake, Sir John Hawkins, Sir Richard Grenville, Captain William Bligh, Captain Tobias Furneaux, Captain Robert Scott [1], Sir Ernest Shackleton

Innovators

Robert Hunt, Stanley Gibbons, William Parker, William Cookworthy, Captain Johnnie Walker, Herchel Smith

Philanthropists & Politicians

Agnes Weston, Leslie Hore-Belisha, Nancy Astor, Michael Foot, David Owen

Engineers & architects

John Smeaton, John Foulston, Francis Fowke, Sir John Rennie, John Rennie Sr, James Rendel, Isambard Kingdom Brunel

Artists

Nicholas Condy, Samuel Prout, Sir Joshua Reynolds, JMW Turner, Beryl Cook [2], Robert Lenkiewicz, George Passmore (of Gilbert & George), David McKee

Performing Arts & Media

Maria Foote [3], Samuel Phelps, Charles Dance, Douglas Hodge, Dawn French, Angela Rippon, Wayne Sleep, Rosie Huntington-Whiteley

Sport

Jack Leslie [4], Trevor Francis, Sharron Davies, Tom Daley, Rūta Meilutytė, Lewis Pugh, Henry Slade

Passing through

Catherine of Aragon, Pocahontas, Captain James Cook, the Emperor Napoleon, Charles Darwin [5], Alexander Selkirk, Sir Arthur Conan Doyle, TE Lawrence of Arabia, Laurel and Hardy, Charlie Chaplin, Winston Churchill, Sir Francis Chichester, the Beatles

Sutton Harbour and the Barbican

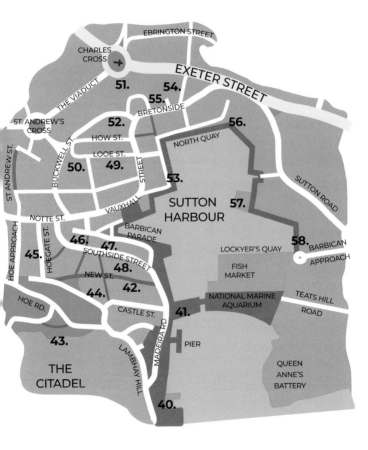

40. PHOENIX WHARF, MADEIRA ROAD

Remnant of former naval victualling yard, and the Emigration Depot

This building at the far end of the Barbican near Fisher's Nose (recently converted into a restaurant) is all that remains of a line of warehouses and wharfside buildings that used to stretch from the point to the Mayflower Steps. This was the Naval victualling yard from the time of Oliver Cromwell. It was here that ship's pursers during the centuries of war with Holland and France would have come ashore to argue with the Victualler's Office about the quantity and quality of the stores provided.

Naval victuallers provided salt pork and beef, butter and cheese, dry food like ship's biscuit and oatmeal, and water, beer and rum. All of this was stored in casks and stowed deep in the ship's hold. To provide the quantity of stores needed, the yard had its own brewery, slaughterhouse, mill and bakehouse, and a cooperage to make the casks. It also supplied cordage and spars, and all the equipment needed by a ship of the line.

Following the construction of the Royal William Yard at Stonehouse in the 1830s, the site at the Barbican became vacant, and the buildings took on a new role as the government's chief Emigration Depot.

Assisted passages were provided by the colonial governments of the Cape, Australia and New Zealand to encourage emigration to the colonies. An account in the *Sydney Mail* in 1885 stated that "Plymouth has always been the leading port for Government emigration, the position being unrivalled as a point of departure, [and] very conveniently situated for the reception of emigrants from Ireland and Scotland, as there are weekly steamers from Dublin, Cork, Waterford, Limerick, and Glasgow, etc. The emigration depot at Plymouth is the only establishment of its kind on any considerable scale in the kingdom, and is admirably adapted for its purposes".

From 1847 to about 1900 some 300,000 to 400,000 emigrants from Ireland, Scotland and the Westcountry embarked here for the colonies – Australia, Canada, the East Indies and the Cape in particular – as well as the United States. Living conditions at the depot were good, but many of the migrants were from homes already hit by unemployment and poverty, and their resistance to disease was weakened by malnutrition. Those who arrived sick were placed in isolation wards, and a report by the Government Emigration Agent in 1852 stated that there would have been more disease and distress without the depot in which the migrants could await their ships.

In 1874 it was said that there were 116,490 English emigrants, 60,496 Irish, 20,286 Scottish, and 43,742 from elsewhere. Of these, most went to the United States. Emigration probably reached its peak in 1878, when there were 15,500 emigrants leaving in 100 ships, with a record exodus of 1,800 in just one week. Many of them were from Cornwall, which was in decline following the steady closure of most of its metal mines in the face of competition from abroad.

41. MAYFLOWER STEPS, THE BARBICAN

Where the Pilgrim Fathers didn't embark on the Mayflower

These old stone steps leading down to the water's edge are known as the Mayflower Steps, in commemoration of the *Mayflower* which sailed from Sutton Harbour on 6 September 1620 with 102 men, women and children, bound for Virginia.

These steps did not exist in 1620. The pier is not shown on any of the seventeenth century maps of Sutton Harbour. No one knows where the pilgrims actually embarked, although Chris Robinson, one of Plymouth's foremost historians, suggests it may have been somewhere in the vicinity of the ladies' lavatories at the nearby Admiral McBride pub, which, admirable as they may be for some purposes, are not a picturesque place of pilgrimage. The likelihood is that the pilgrims embarked into boats which took them out to where the *Mayflower* rode at anchor, and this is the scene which is depicted in the splendid Victorian stained glass window at Sherwell United Church, North Hill.

The Mayflower Pilgrims were not the first English settlers in New England, but they were among the first to survive. Even so, they suffered many calamities. After enduring a terrifying 65-day crossing of the stormy Atlantic, they arrived well to the north of Virginia, landing at a sandy wilderness near Cape Cod in what is now Massachusetts. About half of them died during the long winter from cold, pestilence and starvation. Nevertheless 1620 is taken as the start of the steady European colonisation of North America, and these steps are a reminder of that epic journey.

42. ELIZABETHAN HOUSE, NEW STREET

Reputedly haunted house built in Elizabethan times

The rapid growth of Plymouth during Elizabethan times led to the construction of new houses between Castle Street and the houses and warehouses lining the quay. In mediaeval times the street was known as Greyfriars Street, and later Rag Street, but it appears to have become New Street after the new houses were built. It was laid out by a local merchant and entrepreneur John Sparke, said to be the first Englishman to use and document the South American words 'potato' and 'tobacco'.

Like most streets of the mediaeval and Tudor period, New Street was laid out with 'burgage' plots, with narrow street frontages extending back a long way. To make the most of each plot, the upper floors of most buildings would have been cantilevered out over the street. No 32 New Street is a timber framed building with a party wall of Plymouth limestone, which was built by a local merchant, Richard Brendon, to let out to tenants. Over time, as Plymouth continued to expand, more and more people crowded into the now-decaying tenements of New Street, so that by the mid-Victorian era New Street and the Barbican had become filthy slums, with tenants afflicted by disease and hunger. At one time no less than 58 occupants were said to be living at 32 New Street, and the area was one of the most overcrowded in the country. There was no power to make landlords improve old properties. Refuse and 'night soil' were collected into heaps, where they remained until the rubbish contractors carted it away.

In 1926 the house became subject to a compulsory purchase order requiring the owner to demolish it. The potential loss of such an historic building led to a successful conservation campaign involving the local MP, Nancy Astor, and the newly-formed Old Plymouth Society. In 1930 it was opened to the public as the Elizabethan House, and furnished in the style of the age.

The Elizabethan House retains many of its original features. Its structure and layout are largely unaltered, with bare wooden floors and white lime-washed plaster walls, and six rooms on the three floors and basement connected by a spiral staircase built around a ship's mast. It is planned to tell the story of its past owners and residents, including an Elizabethan merchant, a Georgian businessman and a Victorian washer-woman, with actors and special effects.

The house is reputedly haunted. Many people say they have seen the figure of a young woman wearing a white cap and apron staring back at them through the first floor window. Her outline is so vivid that people often come in from the street and ask who she is. There are also frequent complaints of 'cold spots' inside the house even on a hot summer's day, and some people experience an icy coldness in certain rooms.

Members of staff in the ground floor office have reported hearing furniture dragged around on the building's upper floors, although on inspection nothing is out of place.

43. ROYAL CITADEL GATE, HOE ROAD

England's finest fortress, with its Baroque gatehouse of 1670

The Royal Citadel of Plymouth is said to be the world's oldest fortification in continuous military use. Since it was built, some 450 years ago, it has been a base for guns and gunners protecting the naval port of Plymouth from enemy invasion, and today it is occupied by 29 Commando Regiment Royal Artillery. It is one of Europe's finest fortifications and the country's best-preserved example of a seventeenth century bastioned fortress.

Construction started in 1665, soon after the restoration of Charles II to the throne following the death of Cromwell, and continued until the mid 1670s. At that time the main threat came from the Dutch, who in 1652 had defeated an English fleet off Plymouth, and Anglo-Dutch naval battles continued throughout the late seventeenth century. Perhaps surprisingly, the Citadel was designed by a Dutchman, Sir Bernard de Gomme, who was the King's Engineer-General. The walls were built in stone, backed by deep ramparts of earth and rubble, and incorporating some of the foundations and perhaps even the earthworks of Drake's Fort, which had been built after the rout of the Spanish Armada. Several of the stone arches from the old fort were incorporated into the building.

It is sometimes said that the defensive works and guns facing inland were designed to subdue the town of Plymouth, which had strongly supported Parliament against the King during the English Civil War. However, as any military engineer knows, the landward side is usually the most likely point for an attack, rather than the seaward side whose steep cliffs and rocks make a direct assault difficult, and guns were needed to deter the enemy from placing siege artillery on the north side where it could batter the walls and effect a breech.

The fine Baroque entrance arch dated 1670 is little changed, save that the statue of King Charles II was removed for safe-keeping when William of Orange landed in Torbay in 1688 to overthrow Charles' successor, his brother James II (who unlike Charles II had something of his late decapitated father about him, being Catholic and rather uncompromising). The statue has never been seen since, and was replaced at some point by three cannonballs. The Royal Arms and the decorative panels with suits of armour were originally covered in gilt.

The gatehouse had a drawbridge over a dry moat (the slots and chain-wheels for the drawbridge chains are still evident), with a defensive V-shaped outer wall called a ravelin protecting the gatehouse from artillery. These outer works were removed in the late nineteenth century, but the position of the ravelin is still apparent in the V-shape of the grass triangle which replaced it.

In the 1980s the Citadel was extended to the east at considerable expense to provide room for garaging vehicles and guns, with a massive stone-faced concrete wall in the style of the rest of the Citadel which looms over the Barbican.

44. OLD JEWISH CEMETERY, LAMBHAY HILL

A disused Jewish cemetery, the last resting place of Barney the cat

Behind a plain wooden door not far from the Citadel lies a secret garden – the Old Jewish Cemetery. Contained within high stone walls it has remained hidden from public view for over a century. In 2016 the door was opened and for the first time in its history the public were allowed to step over the threshold.

The caretaker of Plymouth Synagogue, Jerry Sibley, was unaware of it until a complaint about trees affecting a telephone line led him to discover from Google Earth this piece of land, long abandoned. He managed to obtain from the Synagogue a key which fitted the door. What he found was "like a wildlife park", with gravestones poking out of a thick jungle of undergrowth, each one inscribed with Hebrew text.

He cleared the cemetery with the help of some friends. They started getting a few enquiries from tourists who had family connections and wanted to visit their relatives, followed by genealogists who thought they had Jewish ancestors in Plymouth.

Though many of the gravestones are worn away and the text is unreadable, they hold the stories of former inhabitants of Plymouth who lived and died in the eighteenth and nineteenth centuries. The dates are given in the Hebrew calendar which starts in the year 3761 BC, which the 12th-century Jewish philosopher Maimonides established as the biblical date of Creation, although because the Hebrew year varies according to the length of the solar year, dates do not correspond precisely to the Gregorian calendar.

There is an audio trail which describes the lives of some of those who are known to have been buried here. One of the stories is about Barney, Jerry Sibley's cat. Barney took to life at the Synagogue like a rabbi. He always followed Jerry to work and to the services, sitting in the vestry beside the door and watching the congregation coming in and out. As a black and white cat he blended perfectly with the Jewish men in their dark coats and hats and white prayer shawls.

Barney died at Passover. "But there was nowhere to bury him, so when I spoke to some of the committee about it being possible to bury Barney in the old cemetery, they discussed it because it is not really the done thing. They said I had to find a little patch where he could be buried without upsetting anybody. If I could do that then they were happy for it to go ahead".

The whole congregation turned out for Barney's interment in a corner of the cemetery, where Barney's grave is marked by a black headstone. His inscription in white lettering says 'The Guardian of the Threshold'. In the Jewish tradition, small stones are piled on the grave by visitors to honour his memory.

45. CPT. JOHNNIE WALKER'S BIRTHPLACE, HOE GARDENS

Famed U-boat hunter's childhood home

Churchill said that only one thing kept him awake at night during the Second World War - the heavy losses suffered by Allied convoys from German U-boats. The U-boat flotillas under Admiral Donitz became very effective at finding targets in the immensity of the Atlantic and sinking them, so much so that in 1942 alone, 1,664 Allied ships totalling almost eight million tons were lost, most of them to U-boats. The Battle of the Atlantic lasted the entire duration of the war, from September 1939 to May 1945, and the U-boats were the last part of the Nazi war machine to surrender.

Britain was critically dependent on goods imported by sea. Keeping the supply lines open from North America and the West Indies was as important to the nation's survival as had been the Battle of Britain in 1940. Britain was a great manufacturing nation, capable of producing all it needed, but without raw materials and food, its factories would have ground to a halt and its people would have starved. Putting together the resources necessary to take the war to the enemy at D-Day would have been unthinkable without tackling the U-boat menace.

The U-boat's strength lay in its ability to launch torpedoes of immense destructive power while still invisible to its prey. But its great weakness was that it had to surface regularly to enable its diesel engines to generate power for its electric motors, when it was a sitting duck.

No one played a greater part in the containment of the U-boats than Captain Frederick John (Johnnie) Walker of the Royal Navy, born here in 1896. Walker was already 43 when the war started, and it was 1941 before he got his first commission, as commander of a sloop engaged in convoy protection. He made a name for himself by hunting U-boats some distance from the convoy he was protecting. Although the tactic proved remarkably successful, he was regarded as a maverick by Naval High Command, and had to put up with a shore posting until his expertise as an anti-submarine commander came to the notice of the C-in-C of the Western Approaches. At Walker's suggestion he was appointed as commander of a small flotilla of sloops, with the aim of actively seeking out and destroying U-boats rather than merely escorting convoys.

In this role he excelled. His innovative approach to destroying submarines was increasingly successful, and the death in action of his son in 1942 turned the hunting of U-boats into a personal vendetta. He threw everything he had into the task. The strain ultimately proved too much, and he died of a cerebral thrombosis in July 1944. By then, although the Battle of the Atlantic still raged, the U-boat threat had been contained.

By the end of the war, 781 U-boats had been sunk, with the loss of nearly 35,000 of the 38,000 Kriegsmarine personnel serving in the U-boat arm of the German navy.

46. LENKIEWICZ MURAL, BARBICAN PARADE

Robert Lenkiewicz, the Barbican's maverick artist

Almost erased by decay and partly obscured by battens, Robert Lenkiewicz' great Barbican Mural, painted in 1972, is in a sorry state. But the more we look at it, the more faces we see staring out at us. The painter's own face can still be glimpsed beneath the semi-circular window, as if trampled beneath the great crowd above.

"It is to be imagined that a large group of Elizabethan contemporaries numbering a little more than a hundred individuals are walking through an alley flanked by buildings", he wrote. "The theme of the mural concerns itself with metaphysical ideas current in England during the period 1580-1620". These ideas included "philosophy, alchemy, cabala, ceremonial magic, the symbolic aspects of poetry, music and art, the cult of melancholy, chivalry and similar allegorical trends". He wanted to convey a feeling of "the demoniac brilliance of the Elizabethan Age, a time of tremendous skills, flights of imagination, and great brutalities, a time very much like our own".

Lenkiewicz' description of the mural says more about him than about the painting. The range of his interests was wide, and although his output was extensive and his paintings were much in demand, he was always short of money. In part, this was because of his passion for books (especially antique ones) - at his death his library contained more than 25,000 books valued at over £1m, on subjects as diverse as anatomy, the occult, Eastern philosophy and the mediaeval mind. But he was also unfailingly generous with what money he had, and befriended local homeless 'characters', often painting them.

He was fascinated with the power of erotic love both as a subject for study and as a guide to life. He seemed to exert an extraordinary power over women, and had numerous mistresses and at least 17 children by various partners. He cultivated a rather piratical air, with his flowing locks, black cape, red scarf and sea boots, and was instantly recognisable from a long way off.

Almost all his paintings are portraits, including plenty of nudes. Although his work was thought to be rather dated by the artistic establishment of the time, people were drawn to his paintings by the empathy with his subject that shines through them. Like the Barbican mural, some of his paintings were on a vast scale with a throng of people, but each face was painted from life. A large surviving mural by him can be seen at Port Eliot, the home of the Earl of St Germans, who was an admirer of his work and supported him financially.

Lenkiewicz came to feel that his Barbican mural was overshadowing his other work, and he covered it with whitewash, with the addition of three flying ducks. For his project on death he locked himself away and sent notice of his demise to the papers. Incidents like these did much to keep his name at the forefront of Plymouth life until he died for real in 2002, at the age of 61.

47. OLD CUSTOMS HOUSE, BARBICAN PARADE

Probable birthplace of Captain William Bligh of HMS **Bounty**

Poor Captain Bligh! Forever vilified by the 1962 film *The Mutiny on the Bounty,* when he was in truth by no means the cruel tyrant that was portrayed.

He was probably born here in 1754, as his father was the city's customs and revenue officer and this building was the Customs House. Two months before his eighth birthday he was enrolled as 'ship's boy' on HMS *Monmouth*, where he would have learnt the principles of navigation and mathematics, the names of the ropes, sails and spars of a naval warship, and how to climb to the crow's nest. He was commissioned as a lieutenant in 1775.

In 1776 at the age of only 22 he was taken on by the famous Captain James Cook as his sailing master, an extremely challenging and responsible post for a man of his age, given that the *Resolution* was sailing to uncharted seas in the southern Indian Ocean on a voyage that would last for four years. He surveyed many areas including the Sandwich Islands which had not yet appeared on Admiralty charts, and Cook even named an island after him. Cook's death in 1778 left him with sole responsibility for navigation during the last two years of the expedition.

On his return he was now a highly skilled and sought-after navigator, and in 1787 he was chosen to command HMS *Bounty* on a voyage to Tahiti to obtain breadfruit trees, which the botanist Sir Joseph Banks had recommended as a fodder plant suitable to be grown in the Caribbean to feed the slaves working in the sugar plantations. The *Bounty*, specially adapted for the purpose, spent five months in Tahiti collecting and nurturing breadfruit plants. Perhaps (with hindsight) unwisely, Bligh allowed the crew to live ashore, where they enjoyed the somewhat free-and-easy customs of the Tahitians. Some of the seamen had themselves tattooed in the native fashion, and others lived with the famously beautiful and willing native girls. Fletcher Christian, the Master's Mate and Bligh's second-in-command, even took a Tahitian wife.

It is perhaps not surprising that shortly after the *Bounty* left Tahiti many of the crew, led by Christian, mutinied. Life in the South Sea Islands was too idyllic for them to contemplate a return to the rigours of life on board a naval warship. Bligh and those who remained loyal to him were forced into the ship's launch, an open boat just 23ft long, equipped with four cutlasses, a sextant and enough provisions for only five days. It says much for Bligh's leadership and navigation skills that he managed to sail the boat some 3,600 miles through storm and tempest to the Dutch colony of Timor with the loss of only one man, who was killed by natives when they attempted to land on an island to obtain provisions.

Bligh showed more concern for the health of his crew on long voyages than most naval commanders of the time. He was rather unimaginative and stiff in his manner, and always did things 'by the book', but there is no evidence he was either tyrannical or cruel. On the contrary, save where the joys of Tahiti beckoned, he was well-regarded by the crews who sailed with him.

48. JACKA BAKERY, SOUTHSIDE STREET

Britain's oldest commercial bakery dating from about 1587

This unassuming artisan bakery in the Barbican's main street is the oldest commercial bakery in continuous use in the country, and is said to have provided bread for the Puritan pilgrims as they embarked on the *Mayflower* in 1620. It is thought to date from the late 1500s, and may even have been selling bread and pastries in 1588 when the country's fleet assembled in Sutton Harbour for the defence of the realm against the Spanish Armada.

There is a 300-year old oven and other period features, although the building has evolved over the centuries and is very different from what it would have looked like in Elizabethan times. It was run by the Fone family for most of its history, only passing to the Jacka family in the early twentieth century. It remains a family business.

But its history would not always been a peaceful one. In the late 1700s, while war raged with revolutionary France, crops failed and the cost of bread and potatoes rocketed. Riots ensued across the country, and in March 1801 things came to a head in Plymouth. Farmers were the main target, as they could get a much better price for their corn by selling it in London, and some bakers hoarded flour in the expectation that prices would rise even higher. Mobs roamed the streets attacking those they thought responsible for hoarding or profiteering, smashing windows and threatening bakers, farmers and even butchers. Troops were brought in to patrol the streets and restore order.

In Devonport, one Charles Jacob was arrested by the militia for smashing a window, but so enraged was the crowd that they broke into the courthouse and rescued him, smashing the windows of the magistrate's house for good measure.

These were anxious times for the establishment. Revolution was in the air, and the recent French Revolution and the naval mutinies of 1797 made the maintenance of civil order of prime importance. In May 1801 the authorities intervened and sacked 68 dockworkers who were implicated in the unrest. Two men were executed for attacking and damaging a farm near Plympton, and in Taunton two men were executed publicly in the market square for rioting.

Food riots were a frequent occurrence throughout England during much of the eighteenth century, as the growing populations of the towns made people more dependent on shop prices and in particular the cost of flour. At different times and in different parts of the country there were riots and unrest prompted not only by the cost of food, but by low wages, the introduction of machinery and the enclosure of open land. The conditions which led to the storming of the Bastille and the execution of Louis XVI in France were present here also. But England had done with civil war only a century before, and the horrors of the Terror did nothing to encourage a belief that revolution would or could change things for the better.

49. MINERVA INN, LOOE STREET

Claims to be Plymouth's oldest public house and the 'home of the Press Gang'

Among the many Tudor buildings which were saved from the ruthless post-war destruction in and around the city centre is the Minerva Inn, named after Minerva, the multi-tasking Roman goddess of warfare, commerce, medicine, wisdom, and arts and crafts including music, poetry and weaving. The Minerva Inn is said to date from 1540, although others have dated it to the late 1500s or early 1600s.

Although it claims to be Plymouth's oldest public house, there is no evidence it became a pub until long after the nearby King's Head opened its doors in the 1620s.

The Minerva is said to have more than its fair share of ghostly apparitions. There is 'Henry' who has taken to strolling around the bar, before terrifying everyone with a bloodcurdling scream. There is the little girl in a Victorian dress who enters the bar area through a wall, seems to draw some water into a bucket and then vanishes. Then there are the five prostitutes who appear sitting at a table under the dartboard by the original entrance, talking and flirting with unseen sailors.

During the Napoleonic Wars the Minerva was one of the places used by the Press Gang, whose task was to impress men into the Royal Navy's warships moored in the Cattewater. Impressment was used by the Royal Navy in time of war from 1664 until the early nineteenth century as a means of manning its warships. A ship-of-the-line needed a crew of between 500 and 875, crammed into the cramped and stifling 'tween-decks, with hammocks and mess tables slung between rows of heavy cannon. Even a small frigate or sloop needed 200 or more men. Although cruel (and deeply resented), impressment was deemed necessary in order that the Navy could function effectively. Some people did volunteer, but naval service was hard and dangerous, and discipline was harsh, enforced by flogging for minor misdemeanours.

Officially, people liable to impressment by force were 'eligible men of seafaring habits between the ages of 18 and 55 years', but at the height of the Napoleonic Wars over half the 120,000 men serving in British warships were forcibly impressed, and many of them were landsmen with no experience of seafaring at all. Many impressed men were merchant seamen returning to port from a long voyage, or people convicted of petty crimes.

At the Minerva there is a small stairway peephole where it is claimed the press gang would watch for potential recruits entering the establishment, and drop a shilling in their beer. If the unsuspecting patron drank from the glass then they had 'accepted the King's shilling' and were taken off to join the Navy, if necessary accompanied by a blow to the head. An impressed man would have no chance to say goodbye to wife and family. Almost before they realised what was happening, they would be on board ship and subject to naval discipline, the rope's end and the lash.

50. JOHN HAWKINS OF BUCKWELL STREET

Merchant trader who devised the triangular slave trade

The stones of this small arch in Buckwell Street are probably part of Palace Court, a mediaeval monastery where Henry VIII's first bride, Catherine of Aragon, spent her first nights on English soil. The ruins of Palace Court were demolished in the nineteenth century, although an ancient mulberry tree and part of a wall still remain behind the Plymouth College of Art building.

Near here was the family home of John Hawkins, an older cousin of Sir Francis Drake (whose house in Looe Street was nearby), and like him, a merchant and privateer. In 1562 Hawkins made a voyage that was to enter the history books – he was the first to establish the so-called 'triangular slave trade'.

The trading of slaves for manufactured goods from Europe began in the 1400s when the Portuguese and Spanish carried slaves bought in Africa across the Atlantic to work in their plantations and mines in the New World. Slave traders did not generally capture and enslave Africans. They bought them in slave markets from other Africans who had enslaved captives in the constant battles between ethnic groups in West and Central Africa, or from Arab slave traders. Hawkins, however, is credited with being the first to deal in slaves as a trading commodity.

He set off from Plymouth in 1562 for the West African coast with a cargo of muskets, cloth, and other manufactured goods prized by the Africans, and traded them for slaves in the slave markets of Guinea. The second leg of the voyage took him across the Atlantic to the Spanish Main (the Caribbean), where he sold his human cargo for pearls, sugar, leather and other valuables. The third leg brought him back to Plymouth, where he sold these at great profit.

Hawkins was not above capturing black Africans and selling them as slaves in the Caribbean plantations. Yet paradoxically, he was known as a kind and generous man who took great care of his crew's health, and was steady and methodical where Drake was impetuous and hot-headed.

He was appointed Treasurer of the Navy to rid the service of corruption, and obtained a pay increase for sailors, arguing that the best ships needed the best men to man them. As Comptroller of the Navy he was responsible for improving the design of naval ships, reducing the top-heavy superstructure of fore-castles and after-castles which had caused Henry VIII's *Mary Rose* to founder, and designing vessels capable of weathering Atlantic storms. Among his innovations were topmasts which could be removed in strong winds, and sheathing ships' hulls below water in copper plates to protect against the Teredo worm.

In 1571 he became MP for Plymouth, and took part in counter-espionage to help foil the 'Ridolfi plot' to assassinate Queen Elizabeth and put Mary, Queen of Scots, on the throne. He was knighted in 1588 for his part in defeating the Spanish Armada.

51. FORMER TURNBULL'S GARAGE, CHARLES CROSS

The first self-service filling station, built on the site of the first Sunday School

The garage business started by George Henry Turnbull in 1908 is still trading in Plymouth, although it now deals with car radio and camper conversions. The original garage premises at Mill Street were totally destroyed during the Second World War and the firm built a new service station at Charles Cross, which was opened in 1958 by the world champion racing driver Stirling Moss. In order to allow an unobstructed floor area, the building featured an unusual cantilevered canopy. This was Britain's most up-to-date filling station and saw frequent visits from oil industry executives.

The garage installed Britain's first self-service petrol pumps in 1963. Three of the pumps blended various intermediate grades of petrol between Regular and Super (Supermix), while the remaining six delivered standard grades. The nine pumps could handle some 76 cars an hour. With no attendant required to fill tanks for customers, the garage was able to sell petrol at a discount.

It was also the first filling station to be built on the outer edge of a roundabout, and the Ministry of Transport took much persuasion to accept that the location would not interfere with the flow of traffic.

The circular quick service bay (which sadly is the only part remaining – currently a cycle shop) was also unique to Britain. This was opened by Stirling Moss in 1964. Cars drove onto a turntable, and were rotated to an available bay and worked on from a platform on the floor below. Turnbull's boasted a special rolling road which enabled testing and diagnostics to be carried out at speeds of up to 120 mph. A waiting room with a coffee bar allowed customers to watch the work being done, and a ramp to the workshop floor below gave access to a semi-automatic car wash.

Another point of interest about the building is that it was constructed on the site of what had been the first purpose-built Sunday school in the country, the creation of the legendary Vicar of Charles Church, the Reverend Robert Hawker, in 1796. He was concerned about the lack of education afforded to working class children, which he considered led them into a life of crime and debauchery. The Sunday School movement spread across the country so rapidly that by 1800 it was estimated that some 200,000 children had enrolled in Sunday Schools. The building survived the war but was demolished to make way for post-war development.

Charles Church was completed in 1657, and was considered to be one of the finest post-Reformation Gothic churches in the country. It was gutted by fire in the Blitz, and the ruins have been retained as a memorial to the civilians of Plymouth killed during the air-raids.

52. TREVILLE STREET SCHOOL, BRETONSIDE

Where Stanley Gibbons (and stamp collecting) was born

The public mail service was created by Charles I in 1635, but postal charges were high, and had to be paid by the recipient, charged according to the number of pages and the distance travelled. In the 1830s the social reformer Rowland Hill proposed a simplification of the postal system by introducing an adhesive stamp to indicate pre-payment of postage, to be delivered at a flat rate of one penny, regardless of distance.

The Penny Black, introduced in 1840 and showing a portrait of Queen Victoria, was the world's first postage stamp issued by a public postal system. All British stamps still bear a portrait or silhouette of the monarch prominently in the design, and they are the only postage stamps in the world that do not indicate a country of origin.

1840 was also the year in which the inventor of stamp collecting, Edward Stanley Gibbons, was born above his father's chemist's shop at 15 Treville Street. Treville Street was renamed Bretonside after the Second World War, and the only remaining reference to it is this entrance archway to the 'Treville Street Board School' which was opened in 1874. Gibbons' interest in postage stamps appears to have started while he was at secondary school. He owned a book containing stamps for exchange, including a Western Australia penny black and a penny 'Sydney View' of New South Wales.

Gibbons left school at the age of 15 and worked for a short while in the Naval Bank in Plymouth before joining his father's business after the death of his elder brother. His father was happy for him to develop his hobby and allowed him to set up a stamp desk in the chemist's shop, which thus became in 1856 the first shop to deal in used postage stamps. In 1863 he was able to buy a sackful of rare Cape of Good Hope triangular stamps, which are now almost the holy grail of stamp collecting, and in 1865 he issued the world's first stamp catalogue.

Gibbons' stamp business grew steadily as public interest took off, and by the time his father died in 1867 he was more interested in stamp dealing than pharmaceutical work, and in 1872 he moved to what was No.8 Lockyer Street where he carried on his business. He moved to London in 1874, and opened a stamp collector's shop in the Strand. He died a wealthy man in 1913.

He married five times, and strangely each of his wives died at a young age. He remarried soon after each death. With his knowledge of drugs, one is naturally suspicious, but no evidence of foul play is known.

Stamp collecting has become one of the world's most popular hobbies, and some countries (not least the UK) make significant sums from the issue of special limited runs. In 2013 it was estimated that there were 60 million stamp collectors across the globe. Stanley Gibbons Ltd is still the premier stamp dealing business, offering the broadest selection of retail philatelic stock of any store in the world.

53. BROAD GAUGE TRACK, VAUXHALL QUAY

The last surviving section of Brunel's broad gauge

Although he was by no means the chief architect of the Industrial Revolution as he is sometimes portrayed, Isambard Kingdom Brunel was certainly a remarkable man. He was alone among the great civil engineers of the early nineteenth century in excelling in so many fields: ship design, bridge-building, dock engineering, architecture, tunnelling, and railway construction.

His innovations in the design of railways were not always successful. He failed to foresee the extent to which the railway network would expand across the country, designing each railway as if it were a turnpike, with a terminus at each end and no attempt to integrate railway A with railway B even if they shared a common terminus – as did the South Devon Railway and the Cornwall Railway at Plymouth's Millbay Station. As far as he was concerned, each railway was a one-off, and if passengers had to walk from one terminus to another in order to continue their journey (as at Bristol), then that was the natural order of things. The Cornwall Loop – the viaduct enabling trains from North Road Station to travel into Cornwall without reversing at Millbay – was not built until 1876, long after the railway had opened to Penzance.

This innovative approach led him to reject the rather arbitrary track width of 4'8½" used by George and Robert Stephenson which was rapidly becoming the standard gauge, and instead adopt a much wider gauge of 7'0¼" to facilitate faster speeds. Although broad gauge trains were indeed faster and more comfortable, it rapidly became clear that the difficulty caused by the growing need to transfer goods and passengers from 'broad' to 'narrow' gauge wagons and coaches where onward travel was involved was a serious inconvenience, and the broad gauge was phased out, the last rails being lifted in 1892.

The railway tracks around Sutton Harbour were jointly owned by the narrow gauge London & South Western Railway and the broad gauge Great Western, and had therefore to be mixed gauge. This was a three rail system with an outer rail common to both broad and standard gauge stock, and two inner rails set at the appropriate width for each.

Sutton Harbour is believed to be the only place where any remnant of the broad gauge can still be seen in situ. The top photograph shows the short section of broad gauge rail at Sutton Wharf which was left where it crossed the siding leading off to the left. Beyond it, the line of the broad gauge rail can be traced where cobbles have been inserted after it was lifted.

Mixed gauge pointwork was complex, as can be imagined. At Victoria Wharf, just round the corner from Sutton Harbour (see the lower picture), there is still a quantity of mixed gauge trackwork, although all goods are now moved by lorry. This is not, however, a survival from the days of the Great Western: the third rail enabled the Wharf's travelling crane to move around the quayside.

54. NORTH STREET AND BILLA'S BURGH

4,000 year old drovers' route to Dartmoor

Long before the town of Plymouth began to grow from a little fishing harbour on the edge of Sutton Pool in mediaeval times, before the Norman and Saxon invasions, before even the last Roman soldiers were called home in 410 to defend their crumbling empire, back in Celtic, pre-Christian times, there was a little settlement called Billa's Burgh or Bilbrough on the north side of Sutton Pool. It probably lay somewhere near where Hawker's Avenue now runs - a little beach between two streams. Bilbury Street nearby commemorates Plymouth's oldest place name.

There were Neolithic settlers in Plymouth from about 3,000 BC. Stone axe-heads have been found at Thorn Park and Compton. Billa's Burgh is believed to date from the era which we call the Bronze Age, dating from around 2,000 BC.

Inland from the margins of the sea, the country was a thicket of scrub and forest which stone or bronze axes could do little to clear. But up on the high ground of Dartmoor, above the tree line, there were acres of grazing land on which to fatten livestock during the summer months, and the hut circles where the shepherds lived and the pounds where they kept their animals overnight still stand on the moorland slopes. It is sometimes believed that Dartmoor was once covered with trees, but this is based on a misunderstanding of the old name Dartmoor Forest. In mediaeval times a 'Forest' was a royal hunting ground, which explains why much of it still belongs to the Duchy of Cornwall.

To reach these moorland grazing lands from their settlements along the Devon coast, the drovers kept to the tops of the long ridges running south from the moor, where the undergrowth was sparser and there were fewer streams and marshes. There were a handful of these ridge roads running inland from the coast into the heart of the moor, and one of them, still a major trunk road out of Plymouth, was what we now call Tavistock Road.

From Billa's Burgh it ran due north up what is now North Street (which runs from The Swallow in Bretonside almost to the top of North Hill) and along Mutley Plain. From there it more or less followed the course of the old Tavistock Road up onto Roborough Down and on towards Shaugh and Princetown. If you know this road you will see that it keeps to the top of the ridge all the way to Yelverton and beyond.

It is a remarkable thought that the busy traffic thundering north from Mutley Plain up Mannamead Road and past Derriford still follows the twists and turns of the Bronze Age drovers' path laid down over 4,000 years ago. The ruler-straight Roman roads which survive elsewhere are a mere 2,000 years old. There can be very few roads anywhere in the world which have been in continual use for as long as that from North Street to Dartmoor.

55. FORMER FARLEY'S BAKERY, BRETONSIDE

Where Farley's Rusks were first baked

The strong interest in public health and efficient sanitation in late Victorian times prompted efforts to tackle the high rate of infant mortality in the first half of the nineteenth century.

In the 1870s Dr William Eales of Plymouth developed a recipe for a teething biscuit intended to provide the growing infant with proper nutrition. The bakery he asked to produce this biscuit was that run by Mrs Ann Farley and her sons at 5 Exeter Street (now Bretonside). Hence the biscuits were sold as Farley's Rusks, and they have been known by that name ever since.

In 1887 the street was rebuilt, and the Farleys' Bakery moved to No.7 Exeter Street (now 41 Bretonside). The rusks were baked in a separate building at the rear of the shop premises. A blue plaque now marks the building.

When Mrs Farley died, her son Edwin took over the business, but in 1912 he emigrated to Canada. He sold the secret recipe for the rusks to William Bolitho Trahair, a local trader and entrepreneur. W B Trahair produced Farley's Rusks from his grocery premises at Notte Street, selling them under the somewhat quaint slogan of the '4Bs - Bonny Bright Baby Biscuits'. Quality control required that the fingernails of the girls employed in the packaging office be inspected every morning, and staff benefits included having improving stories read to them every lunch time. An ardent Methodist lay preacher, 'W B' required his staff to learn a passage of scripture before considering them for employment.

So secret was the recipe that the door of the dough room was kept locked whenever the mixture was prepared. Tea was used in the mixture to give the rusks their brown colour.

The business prospered to the extent that in 1919 new premises in Woolster Street were acquired to accommodate an electrically driven conveyor-belt oven heated by gas, and other members of the Trahair family joined W B Trahair to form Farley's Infant Food Ltd.

In 1931 a new 'model' factory was built at Torr Lane, Hartley (where the Morrison's supermarket now is), and the smell of baking rusks became a familiar one to traffic passing along Outland Road. Production increased rapidly, and the factory expanded steadily to cope with the demand. Rusks were exported around the world, and many people remember the 'Farleymen' jingle, and the Farley's smiling baby face on packets and even the sides of delivery lorries.

The family business was taken over by Glaxo Laboratories in 1968, but Farley's Rusks continued to be produced at Torr Lane until 1990 when the site was cleared for the supermarket.

Farley's Rusks are now produced by Heinz in Kendal.

56. OLD HORSE WASH, NORTH QUAY

Remains of archway beneath North Quay, Sutton Harbour

Few would notice this part of an old archway beneath the quayside at the east end of North Quay. It is the last remnant of the means of access to the salt water of Sutton Pool for washing horses' hooves.

The benefits of cold seawater in strengthening horses' hooves and in healing the scratching and bruising of their fetlocks have been known about since ancient times. Horses' legs are prone to injury as they are long and slender, and horses used for haulage in particular suffer from muscular strain, tendon injury and laminitis, a painful condition of the hoof which causes severe lameness. The low temperature of the water slows the metabolic response of cells so that they need less oxygen to function and the risk of hypoxic injury is reduced. The saltiness improves the horse's circulation and promotes healing and the development of new tissue.

For centuries, local carters had used a narrow beach at this corner of Sutton Pool as a horse wash, and this arch carried North Quay over the access point. The course of the archway can be seen in the mid-nineteenth century map below.

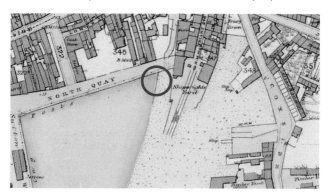

When North East Quay was constructed in 1879 the archway was used to remove spoil and dredged material, before being back-filled with rubble and sealed with masonry.

A small creek was also drained and blocked in constructing North East Quay, and the archway for this is beneath the granite steps leading down to the water.

North Quay retains its railway tracks, and the base for the crane halfway along. *Tiny*, the only surviving original broad gauge locomotive, now preserved at Buckfastleigh, was built for shunting work in Sutton Harbour by Sara & Co of Penryn, Falmouth in 1868.

57. THE CHINA HOUSE, SUTTON HARBOUR

Historic warehouse associated with Cookworthy's English porcelain

The China House has been many things in its long life: warehouse, factory, hospital, prison, shipbuilding store and restaurant. It was built in about 1650 by John Rattenbury for use as a warehouse, but in 1667 the building was bought by the Admiralty for use as a naval victualling storehouse. Later it was used for naval ordnance, and later again as a naval hospital. It is claimed to be the oldest surviving waterside warehouse in the country, and is one of the few remaining with water lapping against three sides.

William Cookworthy was a scientist (or 'natural philosopher'), born in 1705, who became interested in Chinese porcelain manufacture. Chinese porcelain was greatly valued in Europe, and although Europeans had tried to reproduce the process over the centuries, they had never succeeded in producing a porcelain as strong, pure and translucent as 'china'.

It was known that kaolin (china clay) was used in the making of porcelain, and in 1745 Cookworthy found a rare type of decomposed granite known as moorstone. It took him twenty years to find a way to refine it and to develop a process for making porcelain, but it proved to be far superior to that used in the pottery towns around Stoke-on-Trent. He was the first European to produce hard porcelain which was as good as genuine Chinese.

In 1768 he established the 'Plymouth China Works' based at the China House, which was used as a factory for producing and storing his Plymouth porcelain. His wares were displayed and sold from his home in Notte Street. The blue and white patterned Plymouth porcelain became highly popular and was responsible for the beginnings of the china clay industry in Devon and Cornwall. However, a shortage of skilled labour in Plymouth soon forced the business to move eastwards to Bristol, and in the 1780s the business closed, unable to compete with the production of porcelain in the Staffordshire Potteries and elsewhere.

St Austell in Cornwall had the largest deposits of china clay which had then been found anywhere in the world, and by the 1850s 65,000 tonnes a year of clay were being quarried, and 7,000 people were employed in the industry. In 1910 Cornwall was producing about half the world's china clay. There were also large deposits at Lee Moor, near Plymouth, and their conical spoil-heaps and deep flooded quarries continue to dominate the area.

In the early 1990s the China House underwent a substantial but sensitive make-over in order to transform it from a warehouse into a restaurant.

Examples of Plymouth porcelain can be seen at Plymouth Museum.

58. LOCKYER'S QUAY AND JOHNSON'S QUAY

Where Dartmoor granite was brought by horse tramway

The Plymouth & Dartmoor Railway, a horse tramway from Princetown to Sutton Harbour, opened throughout in 1825, the year which also saw the opening of the world's first steam railway, the Stockton & Darlington. It was the brain-child of Sir Thomas Tyrwhitt, who had conceived a scheme to bring the wild slopes of Dartmoor under cultivation, and to that end built himself a country house in 1785 at Tor Royal, near Two Bridges, and founded the settlement of Prince's Town (now Princetown). Both were named in honour of the Prince of Wales, the titular owner of much of Dartmoor. However, the soil proved to be too poor for cultivation, so Tyrwhitt came up with a different plan – to build a prison at Princetown to house French prisoners of war. This grim gaol was built between 1806 and 1808 using granite and moorstone from local quarries.

The end of hostilities in 1815 left the prison empty, and so the indefatigable Tyrwhitt next proposed a horse-drawn tramway from Cattedown to Princetown in order to carry up lime and manure to improve the Dartmoor soil, and to convey down to Plymouth granite and other products which he hoped in time would be produced at Princetown. To build a railway of over 25 miles in such difficult terrain was an ambitious project, but it was supported by local landowners and Plymouth businessmen, and the Act of Incorporation of the Plymouth & Dartmoor Railway (P&DR) was passed in 1819. It was completed in stages, eventually reaching Johnson's Quay at Sutton Harbour in 1825.

Much of the impetus for completing the tramway came from the Johnson Brothers, who owned granite quarries at King's Tor, Swell Tor and Foggintor, and had a contract to supply stone for the Breakwater (and later for London Bridge). When the contractors building the line proved unreliable, the Johnsons undertook to complete it on the basis that the construction costs would be offset against the charges made by the P&DR for the carriage of granite. In the event, the carriage of granite from the quarries around Princetown proved to be virtually the tramway's only source of traffic, so that while the Johnsons were able to bring granite down from the moor to their private quay at Coxside free of charge, the company was left with virtually no income. This was a cause of difficulty and friction as long as the P&DR was in existence. The tramway finally expired in 1883 when the GWR opened its branch line from Yelverton to Princetown using much of the P&DR trackbed.

Lockyer's Quay was built by Edmund Lockyer, who was a founding director of the Plymouth & Dartmoor Railway and later became Mayor of Plymouth. Members of the Lockyer family appear regularly on Plymouth's list of mayors from 1803 to 1844, and have given their name to Lockyer Street. The quay was built in 1833 in order to handle stone from Cann Quarry near Plym Bridge, to which a branch of the P&DR had been opened. Since then Lockyer's Quay has been used at different times as a copper ore yard, a lead factory, a works dealing in concrete, cement and manure, and a coal wharf. It is now the Barbican Fish Market.

Stonehouse

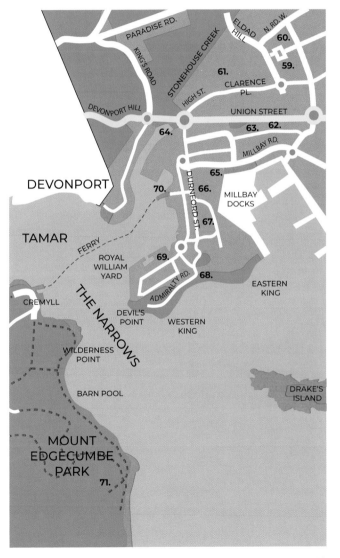

59. ST PETER'S, WYNDHAM SQUARE

State-of-the-art church interior

I n 1830 a non-conformist chapel was built here on what was then open land, close to the Royal Naval Hospital. It was called Eldad Chapel after an obscure character in the Old Testament, and gave its name to Eldad Hill which runs down to Millbridge, where there was once a tide mill. The area around had been developed as we see it now, with the chapel in the centre of a square designed by John Foulston.

In 1848 the chapel was licensed as an Anglican church, and the Reverend George Prynne was appointed Vicar of the new parish of St Peter's. He remained there until his death in 1903. A small chancel was added in 1849-50 by G E Street, who was a prominent church architect, and between 1880-82 the old chapel was completely rebuilt in a restrained Gothic style by G Fellowes Prynne, the son of the vicar. The fine tower was added in 1906.

Father Prynne (as he liked to be known) was a leading member of the Anglo-Catholic movement, and during his 55-year incumbency he championed the Sacrament of Penance and the daily Eucharist in the Church of England. St Peter's remains staunchly Anglo-Catholic, with services more reminiscent of a Roman Catholic church than an Anglican one.

St Peter's was hit by incendiaries during an air-raid on the night of the 21st April 1941 and was completely gutted. It was rebuilt in the 1950s with flat roofs replacing the previous pitched roofs, but the work was of poor standard, and the roof leaked. In 2007 the exterior was repaired and the interior re-ordered at considerable expense, with the assistance of a generous grant from the Whitbread Trust. The resulting building is exceptional.

A striking feature of Harris MacMillan's design is the 30 metre diameter ring of running water under glass which encircles the nave seating. Clever water engineering makes the water appear to flow from the lectern around to the baptismal pool. A combination of filtration, bromination and ozone treatment keeps the water crystal clear, and cooling the water with a heat pump prevents condensation on the underside of the glass. The 'rill' is lit with fibre optic lighting.

The baptismal pool is designed for total immersion, and is covered by removable glass panels across which you walk as you enter the building. Glass is also used for the floor of the circular dais under the east window, and the kitchen area is glassed off to the full height of the nave arches.

Equally striking is the new organ by the Devon organ builder Michael Farley. The pipework is housed in a stainless steel cylinder seemingly suspended in mid air in the west gallery beneath the church tower. The organ console is unusual too, with a tubular frame designed by the architects and a hydraulically adjustable bench.

60. SEWER VENTING CHIMNEY, WYNDHAM LANE

Probably the only large sewer venting chimney to remain in use

1858 was a fine summer, hot and humid. Parliament was sitting in the splendid new gothic-style House of Commons, debating health. The Thames had slowed to a trickle, and the smell of rotting faeces and industrial waste from the river mud banks was so overpowering that MPs had to adjourn to escape the appalling stench. This was 'the Great Stink'. As they had in mediaeval times, the sewers simply poured untreated sewage into the Thames. Three outbreaks of cholera prior to the Great Stink had been blamed on the 'miasma' emanating from the river.

The gradual introduction of flushing toilets in the 1850s only worsened the problem, as they replaced privies draining into a cess pit or soak-away with soil pipes, which washed effluent into the nearest stream or drain.

Joseph Bazalgette, as the chief engineer of the London Metropolitan Board of Works, was given the task of revolutionising London's sewerage system, and under his guidance an extensive enclosed sewerage system was constructed, using pumping stations where the natural flow of water was insufficient. The Embankments north and south of the river were built (using granite from the quarries around Princetown), so that large covered sewers could be installed beneath the pavement to prevent fouling of the Thames. Other cities began to pay more attention to public health and to construct sewerage systems of their own.

In Plymouth, public health in the 1840s was said to be the worst in Europe apart from Warsaw. An enquiry in 1852 reported that in the worst of the slums over 100 people lived in just 16 rooms, sharing a single privy and one tap. In many of these courtyards the cess pools were overflowing, with stinking sewage seeping over the flagstones. Only a few streets had any sort of proper drainage.

Nevertheless Plymouth was among the last to modernise. It was not until the 1880s, after the passing of the Public Health Act in 1875, that mile after mile of enclosed sewer pipes were laid around the city.

Sewage emits a noxious gas, mainly hydrogen sulphide which gives off a smell of rotten eggs. This gas is flammable and corrosive, so the enclosed sewers had to be vented, using venting pipes tall enough to allow the noxious fumes to dissipate above street-level. There are several cast-iron 'stink pipes' looking like truncated lamp-posts on Mutley Plain, the Barbican and elsewhere.

The Wyndham Lane sewer venting chimney was built to ventilate the Dead Lake Sewer. It is unusual because of its great size, and because it is believed to be the only venting chimney in existence which still performs its original function. It continues to be maintained by South West Water.

Nowadays the problem of sewage gas is alleviated by means of vents on top of the soil pipes carrying away effluent from individual houses.

61. FORMER ROYAL NAVAL HOSPITAL, STONEHOUSE

The first hospital designed on hygienic principles, built in about 1758

The birth of Horatio Nelson in 1758 coincided with the birth of the Royal Naval Hospital Stonehouse, the first hospital to be purpose-built on hygienic principles. It provided dedicated care for sick and injured seamen serving in the Royal Navy and became fully operational by 1762. The hospital housed 1,200 patients in sixty wards, in a group of ten ward blocks connected by a colonnade forming a large quadrangle. A central block with a cupola contained the offices and dispensary. The site was surrounded by officers' accommodation, together with a chapel and an octagonal stone water tower at the eastern end, all enclosed within a high stone wall (believed to have been built to prevent sailors deserting whilst in hospital). Apart from one of the ward blocks which was destroyed in 1941, the original buildings survive much as they were built.

The first patients arrived at the Royal Naval Hospital in 1760 during the Royal Navy's 'Year of Victories' in the Seven Years' War, the first truly global war involving conflicts across the world from Europe to India and Canada to the Philippines. Patients were landed by boat at a small quay in Stonehouse Creek, which still survives (although the creek was filled in during the 1960s and early '70s, and is now playing fields).

The design of the hospital was revolutionary, enabling patients with different types of disease or injury to be segregated to reduce the risk of contamination and cross-infection.

The architect was Alexander Rowehead (or Rovehead or Rouchead) who was a master mason from London. Nothing much is known about him, but his design was extremely influential and was adopted in many subsequent hospital buildings, military and civilian. It was promoted by the redoubtable Florence Nightingale a century later as the 'pavilion' pattern. The Stoke Military Hospital across the Creek (now Devonport High School for Boys), built in the 1790s, is similarly arranged in segregated ward blocks. It is said that RNH Stonehouse was the inspiration for Thomas Jefferson's supremely elegant design for the campus of the University of Virginia in Charlottesville.

The Royal Navy's hospital at Portsmouth, RNH Haslar, which on completion in 1754 was the largest hospital in England and the largest brick building in Europe, was designed in a more conventional seventeenth century style, with substantial blocks forming a U-shape as at Greenwich Hospital.

RNH Stonehouse served the Royal Navy for 235 years, from the Seven Years' War and the Battle of Trafalgar, through two World Wars to the Battle for the Falklands in 1982 and the Gulf War of 1990-1991. It dwindled in importance following the completion of Plymouth's integrated hospital at Derriford, and the last departments were moved there in March 1995. The site remained empty for a time, before being converted into luxury apartments with some commercial premises and a school, together forming a secure gated community.

62. PALACE THEATRE, UNION STREET

Landmark late Victorian Music Hall, now derelict

Of all the landmark buildings in Plymouth which survived the Blitz, few can have suffered such ill luck as the Palace Theatre. Completed in September 1898 as a music hall specialising in exotic productions, it could seat 2,500 people. No expense had been spared on the flamboyant exterior design featuring scenes of the Spanish Armada, with eclectic features such as the curious lighthouse at the east corner, or the lavish interior fittings and decoration with plasterwork featuring ships' lanterns, shields, swords, flags and wreaths.

Three months later, the rear of the building including the stage and much of the auditorium was destroyed by fire (said to have been caused by the too-hot muzzle of a cannon used in the evening's performance of 'The Battle of Trafalgar' setting a curtain alight). The theatre was reopened in May 1899 as the New Palace Theatre of Varieties, with a rather less elaborate interior.

The Palace hosted a number of well-known entertainers in its heyday, among them Lillie Langtree, Houdini, Charlie Chaplin, Tommy Handley, Billy Cotton and Louis Armstrong. It hosted Laurel and Hardy's last stage performance on 17 May 1954 – a mild heart attack on Ollie's part meant that the rest of the tour had to be cancelled, and they never performed again in public.

Although it survived the Blitz and underwent a refurbishment in 1949, the great days of touring shows were coming to an end after the Second World War, and tastes in entertainment were changing. The theatre closed in 1954 and was offered for sale to Plymouth City Council, but the council was not interested. Occasional performances continued until 1962, when pantomimes and amateur productions were staged, but in 1965 it was sold to a company which staged wrestling, striptease and bingo events. In 1977 it was restored as a theatre, hosting plays, musicals and pantomimes, as well as performances by Norman Wisdom, Tommy Cooper, Wayne Sleep, Rod Hull and Danny La Rue amongst others.

In 1983 it started a new life as a nightclub, the Academy Disco (later the Dance Academy). This was one of the country's top dance and music venues, capable of accommodating 1,300 dancers. It had a national reputation for so-called 'trance' music and 'hard house' under its resident DJ, Tom Costelloe, and allegedly had more than 20,000 members in 2005. But in 2006 Costelloe and the owner, Manouchehr Bahmanzadeh, were arrested for permitting the premises to be used for the 'blatant' supply of ecstasy, a Class A drug, and both were given lengthy prison sentences. The building remains empty and increasingly derelict, despite efforts to bring it back to life – an 'at risk' listed building, with a fine crop of something growing from the parapets and chimneys.

The theatre is reputedly haunted. In the 1980s two security guards doing their rounds in the early morning heard a woman scream, and the lights went out. It is said that strange noises and the appearance of dark silhouettes resembling people have been seen in areas which were unoccupied at the time.

63. GENESIS BUILDING, UNION STREET

Stonehouse regeneration project's business centre, with 'living walls'

Union Street was designed by the great Plymouth architect of the early 1800s, John Foulston, and was laid out between 1812 and 1820 as a 'grand boulevard' to unite the three towns of Plymouth, East Stonehouse and Devonport. It comes as a surprise to us now, but for much of the nineteenth century it was a fashionable street, and was seen as a welcome embellishment to the town.

But towards the end of the century the tide went out in Union Street, and what had been a fashionable and elegant area became Plymouth's red light district, with prostitutes and drinking clubs and sailors having a 'good time'. In the '60s and '70s, evenings in Union Street usually saw the Naval Provost's Land Rovers on hand, helping to ferry away the inebriated and attempt to maintain some sort of order. Much of Union Street has been redeveloped, while parts of it are lined with decaying shops and clubs, interspersed with used furniture stores and a few remaining specialist traders. An Aldi and a Lidl have brought more customers, but it nevertheless seems a surprising place to come across Plymouth's most energy-efficient office building, with its living wall containing 18,600 plants and carved reliefs depicting artisans at work.

The Genesis Business Centre was opened by HRH the Princess Royal in June 2015, and has won many awards, including 'Building of the Year' from the Building Forum for Devon & Cornwall. It was built by the Millfields Trust, a social trading enterprise working in partnership with Plymouth City Council, local businesses and the community, to help regenerate Union Street and Stonehouse (an area which needs all the help it can get). It owns four premises, which are designed to encourage business enterprise, mainly emerging and small to middling organisations in the service sector including charities and the creative arts. Its 'Millfields Inspired' project aims to inspire young people by giving them an experience and a taste for the world of work, to assist them when they come to consider their choice of career.

The Genesis Building was designed by Graham Lobb, a Plymouth-born architect who has designed many of the city's best-known and innovative buildings in regeneration areas like the Barbican, Sutton Harbour, Devonport and Stonehouse. His award-winning buildings include the Nelson Project, Salt Quay House in Sutton Harbour, the Barbican Glassworks (now the Harbour Seafood Restaurant) and George House, as well as the Genesis Building.

The bas-relief panels were designed by Richard Fisher and sculpted by Jonathan Sells. They depict rather Peruvian-looking artisans at work, sawing and shaping timber, boatbuilding, quarrying stone and breaking up limestone for burning in limekilns. These are all trades associated with Stonehouse in former times. Limestone from Plymouth was carried up river by barge and unloaded at riverside quays, where it was burnt in kilns to produce fertiliser. One panel shows tree trunks being seasoned by immersing them in sea water, a process which was carried out in Stonehouse Creek.

64. STONEHOUSE BRIDGE AND TOWN WALL

Georgian toll bridge of 1773 and surviving section of mediaeval town wall

Unnoticed and uncared for, Smeaton's stone bridge over Stonehouse Creek now lies beneath a busy dual carriageway, its archway blocked following the filling in of the creek above the bridge in about 1972.

The bridge was opened in 1773 as a toll bridge, paid for by the local Lords of the Manors of East Stonehouse and Stoke Damerel, to replace the foot ferry which had been the only means of crossing the creek at Stonehouse. As the toll for pedestrians was a halfpenny, the bridge was always known as 'Ha'penny Bridge'. The tolls were not removed until 1924 when the bridge was adopted by Plymouth Town Council.

Originally the bridge was humped - the outline we see today dates from 1828 when the approaches were raised using blank arches, to make it easier for hackney carriages and coaches to surmount the bridge. During the course of the work a Roman-style charnel house was discovered, with crypts or chambers containing charred human remains. It has been speculated that this (or some other Roman building in the vicinity) gave Stonehouse its name, since the early Saxon settlers must have found a substantial stone-built house here for them to name it so, and stone houses were rare after Roman times outside the larger towns.

Further into Stonehouse, next to the Citroen car showroom, stands one remaining section of the mediaeval town wall. Although the north side is difficult to access and very overgrown, it is possible to see the banquette or firing step, seemingly on the wrong side of the wall. Surely the defenders would have been looking out to the north, not the south? But although today much of what we think of as Stonehouse lies to the south, stretching along Durnford Street to Devil's Point and the Royal William Yard, in mediaeval times the town lay to the north, between the wall and the bridge. As well as a church, a manor house and a town hall, a 'bird's eye' map of the area of 1540 shows a town wall with a small fort, a turret and a gatehouse, with openings for cannon. A deer park is shown to the south of the wall.

East Stonehouse, as it used to be (West Stonehouse, destroyed by the French in a raid in 1350, was on the Cornish side of the Tamar, where Cremyll is now), was one of the 'Three Towns' incorporated into the borough of Plymouth in 1914, and it has a long history. It grew slowly from Saxon times until the Royal Naval Hospital and Royal Marine Barracks were built in the latter half of the eighteenth century, when it grew rapidly. The old lane wandering along the peninsula to the Cremyll ferry (which then ran from Devil's Point, closer to the west bank of the Tamar) became Durnford Street, then a fashionable residential area and now regaining something of its former glory, and development continued to the east. After the Second World War the remains of the old town including the East Stonehouse Brewery were steadily demolished, and its foundations now lie under the sprawling sheds of Princess Yachts.

65. CAROLINE PLACE, STONEHOUSE

The birthplace of Cora Pearl, the greatest courtesan of 19th century Paris

Emma Eliza Crouch was born in Caroline Place, Stonehouse in 1835 (probably), although she later claimed to have been born in 1842. She became one of the most famous and successful courtesans of the French Second Empire.

Her parents were singer-musicians working in Plymouth's many theatres and music halls. Earning a living on the stage was always a hand-to-mouth existence, and life was hard. After selling one of his compositions for the substantial sum of £5, her father abandoned his family and sailed for America, where he bigamously remarried. It seems that the teenage Emma became so unruly she was sent to a convent school in Burgundy, where she was taught the French language, deportment and etiquette as befitted a young lady.

On her return she moved to London to live with her grandmother, and took a job as a milliner's assistant. It was not uncommon for attractive young shop girls to earn easy money by occasional prostitution, and Emma seems to taken full advantage of her good looks. She became the mistress of Robert Bignell, an outwardly respectable wine merchant who was also proprietor of what we would now call a nightclub. On a trip together to Paris, Emma saw her chance to leave her past behind and enter into high society. She declined to return to London with Bignell and changed her name to the rather more exotic Cora Pearl.

Her first major conquest in 1860 was Francois Victor Massena, the Duke of Rivoli and Prince of Essling, a descendant of one of Napoleon Bonaparte's Marshals, who lavished gifts and fine clothes on her. By the time he died three years later Cora was firmly established as a 'demi-mondaine', a fashionable courtesan attracting an admiring crowd (of men) wherever she went. Such was her allure that she could command up to 10,000 francs a night, at a time when a skilled craftsman would be paid just two francs a day. SOme of her most exuberant acts involved dancing nude on a carpet of orchids, arriving on stage dressed in nothing but a thick layer of cream, and bathing before dinner guests in a silver tub full of champagne.

In 1868 she achieved her greatest conquest, Prince Jerome Napoleon, cousin and close adviser to the Emperor. Her jewellery collection was valued at a million francs, not to mention her horses, houses and dresses. She is said to have once received a lingerie bill for over 5,000 francs, about £18,000 now.

Her fall came with the Franco-Prussian War of 1870. While the wealthy fled abroad, Cora stayed on in Paris and, during the four-month siege of the city, cared for the wounded, fed the starving and gave shelter to the needy. By the end of the conflict everything had changed. The ostentatious opulence of the Second Empire was no longer in vogue, and with her attractions waning she was forced to sell everything to settle a string of debts. In 1886 she had to move to a shabby tenement where she died of cancer in poverty and obscurity. She is buried in Batignolles Cemetery as plain Emma Crouch.

66. ROYAL MARINE BARRACKS, DURNFORD STREET

The last survivor and the finest of Plymouth's many barracks

The Royal Navy's infantry division was established in 1755 as 'His Majesty's Marine Forces', although there had been a 'Maritime Regiment of Foot' as far back as 1664. Marines served a dual function: providing sentries on board ship and generally assisting the officers in maintaining discipline, and taking a leading role in sea-based landings and ship-to-ship engagements. While the seamen would run barefoot to deal with the multitude of tasks aboard a sailing ship of the line, the measured tread of the Marine's hob-nailed boots provided a reassuring sense of solid military discipline.

The value of the Royal Marines as an adaptable fighting force capable of carrying out surprise attacks from the sea became increasingly recognised during the latter part of the nineteenth century, and they took part in many of the skirmishes necessary to keep the Empire under British control. This process culminated in the formation of the Commandos during the Second World War. Royal Marine Commandos are now regarded as among the most effective and versatile fighting forces on the globe, and they are the only force in Europe capable of conducting amphibious operations at brigade level.

The main part of Stonehouse Barracks was constructed between 1779 and 1785, and comprised a rectangular parade ground set at an angle to Durnford Street, with buildings on three sides. Until about 1870, when the present guardhouse and flanking buildings were added, the Durnford Street side consisted of railings with a small central guardhouse. The eighteenth century buildings are among the oldest of their kind in the country.

Historic England describes Stonehouse Barracks as "the oldest and most important group of barracks in England not forming part of a fortification: a very rare example of eighteenth century planning, and a complex of great historic value". The complex includes a small but perfectly formed theatre, built in about 1788 as a racquets court and converted to a theatre (the Globe Theatre) in about 1830. It hosts occasional events open to the public.

Stonehouse Barracks are the last of the many barracks in Plymouth to survive in military use. Plumer, Seaton, Mount Wise, Raglan, Granby, Cumberland, Mutley, Mill Bay, Elphinstone – all of them have now disappeared.

The Longroom nearby was designed by Sir Robert Taylor in 1756 as an assembly room and the centrepiece of the Mill Bay pleasure grounds, where the great and the good would convene for balls and social functions, or to partake of a little sea bathing at the baths. It has been many things since then: an officers' mess, hospital, school, and an American GI base. It is now the barracks gym. It has lent its name to the Queen's Harbour Master's Longroom Port Control Centre which controls ship movements in and out of the Sound, with an Incident Control Room which deals with all maritime emergencies in the Western Approaches.

67. DURNFORD STREET RESIDENTS

Where Conan Doyle practised as a GP, and Captain Hardy lived

Sir Arthur Conan Doyle qualified as a doctor in 1881 at the University of Edinburgh, and served as medical officer on board a cargo vessel before joining his former classmate George Turnavine Budd at his medical practice at what was No.1 Durnford Street. Dr Budd was extremely eccentric, with unconventional ideas as to treatment. A girl with an annoying cough was put on the mantelpiece and warned that if she coughed again she would fall off into the fire. After an abortive attempt by Dr Budd to cure a man with lockjaw by trying to make him laugh (using an innovative medical procedure involving throwing food at each other), Conan Doyle tired of his associate and travelled to Southsea with only £10 in his pocket. There he set up in practice on his own, having lasted in Durnford Street for less than six months.

Conan Doyle wrote of his experiences with Dr Budd in The Stark Munro Letters published in 1894/5. In his autobiography he said "The whole history of my association with the man whom I called Cullingworth, his extraordinary character, our parting and the way in which I was left to what seemed certain ruin, were all as depicted ... Cullingworth's antics are beyond belief. I laughed until I thought the wooden chair under me would have come to pieces. He roared, he raved, he swore, he pushed [his patients] about, slapped them on the back, shoved them against the wall, and occasionally rushed out to the head of the stair to address them en masse. At the same time, behind all this tomfoolery, I, watching his prescriptions, could see a quickness of diagnosis, a scientific insight, and a daring and unconventional use of drugs, which satisfied me that he was right in saying that, under all this charlatanism, there lay solid reasons for his success."

Durnford Street's brief association with Sherlock Holmes' creator is celebrated in quotes from his books on brass plaques set into the pavement.

Another famous inhabitant of Durnford Street was Captain Thomas Hardy, who commanded HMS *Victory* at the Battle of Trafalgar in 1805. Hardy had served as a lieutenant under Nelson in 1796, and Nelson thought so highly of him that he promoted him Commander and later Captain. Hardy served as Nelson's Flag Captain in the *Vanguard*, *Foudroyant* and *St George* before the *Victory* became Nelson's flagship in 1803. He was on the quarterdeck of the *Victory* when Nelson was hit by a well-aimed French musket ball and carried below, and after the battle was able to tell the dying Nelson of the successful outcome. After asking Hardy to take care of 'my dear Lady Hamilton', Nelson murmured "Kiss me, Hardy". Poor Hardy was forever after known as 'Kiss-me Hardy'.

Hardy had a distinguished naval career, becoming First Lord of the Admiralty in 1830 and Governor of Greenwich Hospital in 1834. His mother lived at what is now No 156 Durnford Street, although a letter written by him in 1818 is addressed from No 42. It is likely that Hardy and his wife took lodgings in what was then a fashionable area whenever the exigencies of naval life took them to Plymouth.

68. GUN BATTERIES, ADMIRALTY ROAD

Gun emplacements defending Plymouth for five centuries

In the late 1400s, a series of wars between the Venetian Republic and the Ottoman Empire had closed the Mediterranean to the lucrative trade with the 'Indies', and prompted a search for alternative routes to reach the spices of the East. The Portuguese sailed into the Indian Ocean around the Cape of Good Hope in 1487, and in 1492 Columbus sailed across the Atlantic on behalf of the Spanish to find a new route to the spice producing regions of the Orient (thereby accidentally discovering the New World). But the English were too busy fighting the French to involve themselves much with exploration until the sixteenth century.

There were periodic raids on Plymouth by the French throughout the late Middle Ages, and in the 1490s and early 1500s Plymouth built a chain of batteries from Mount Edgcumbe at the mouth of the Tamar to Fisher's Nose at the entrance to Sutton Harbour. They are shown in a bird's-eye map of the town of about 1540, with a defensive wall stretching from a fort on the east side of Mill Bay to one at Fisher's Nose. Further protection was given to shipping in Sutton Harbour by a chain which could be raised between two moles near to the Mayflower Steps.

A fort differs from a battery in that a fort is a defensive position such as a castle or stronghold, while a battery merely has firing positions for artillery.

One of the earliest and best-preserved of these batteries is the Artillery Tower at Firestone Bay. From the sea it appears to be a substantial octagonal fortress, although from behind it is unprotected. Gun ports in the lower floors enabled cannon to fire on vessels approaching the mouth of the Tamar. It became obsolete after the construction of the Citadel in the late seventeenth century, and at various times since then it has been used as a police house, coastguard station, MOD store and public lavatory. It is now a well-regarded restaurant.

The tower at Devil's Point also remains, although bricked up and in a poor state. At low tide the gun ports can be seen from the rocks below, together with the defensive wall abutting it. It was probably built by the Earl of Mount Edgcumbe on the orders of Henry VIII at about the same time as the fort on the opposite side of the river at Barn Pool.

Between the Artillery Tower and Devil's Point lies Western King Redoubt, an open battery originally built in 1779 to provide firing positions for eight cannon. At various times since then it has been remodelled and enlarged, and it continued to be used for defensive purposes right up to the Second World War. In 1941 twin 6-pounder Quick Firing guns were placed there to protect the Hamoaze from enemy motor torpedo boats. These guns remained until 1956 when the coastal artillery was removed.

There is much of interest along this short stretch of coast, including a small shingle beach and a seawater bathing pool.

69. ROYAL WILLIAM YARD, STONEHOUSE

Georgian splendour to rival that of Greenwich

The growth of the Royal Navy during the Napoleonic War and the various conflicts which preceded it severely overstretched the cramped victualling yard at Sutton Harbour. As more and more dockyard facilities were based in the Hamoaze at Devonport, it was decided to build a new victualling yard there. The Hamoaze was better protected from storms and from attack than the Cattewater, although the Narrows made access difficult for large sailing vessels, particularly at spring tides.

The site chosen was the peninsula at the mouth of the Tamar known as Passage Point (also known as Cremyll Point and Devil's Point), which then contained little except St Lawrence's Chapel, the ferry crossing to Mount Edgcumbe and some grazing land.

The first part to be built was Clarence Wharf, named after the Duke of Clarence (later King William IV) who laid a foundation stone in 1827. To build the rest of the yard it was necessary to quarry into the hill, and the high cliff behind the yard shows the extent of the excavation. The excavated stone was used to extend the site to about 16 acres by filling in part of Stonehouse Pool. Parts of the old chapel were used in building the Folly at Mount Edgcumbe Park.

The scale and elegance of the yard buildings, echoing the grandeur of Greenwich, comes as something of a surprise to those who see it for the first time. This, after all, was not built for public display, but simply to provide facilities for provisioning the fleet. The buildings were designed by the famous architect, Sir John Rennie, who was also engaged with completing the Breakwater in Plymouth Sound. The government provided what was then the colossal sum of £2 million towards the cost of the work.

The yard is entered through a grand archway surmounted by a statue of William IV. It contained flour mills, a bakery, a brewhouse for making beer, a slaughter-house and butchery, and cooperages where casks were made, to be filled with salted beef, ship's biscuit or beer. In the centre, beneath a fine clock tower, is the harbour or basin where barges would be loaded to carry the casks out to ships moored in the Hamoaze.

At the south east corner of the yard is a seemingly pointless arch beneath Admiralty Road, roofed and floored in cut stone. At its seaward end it simply drops down to the beach below. This was built to enable cattle to be herded straight into the yard from vessels in Firestone Bay via a pontoon, although there is no evidence it was ever used for this purpose. It is rumoured that the tunnel was used to store the Belgian Crown Jewels during the First World War.

The yard continued in use for fleet victualling until the 1970s, thereafter serving as storage for military equipment. It was officially closed in 1992, and ownership transferred to the Plymouth Development Corporation. It is now a busy 'village' with apartments, restaurants, galleries and pop-up shops.

70. ADMIRAL'S HARD & CREMYLL FERRY

Passenger ferry across the Tamar to Mount Edgcumbe Park

There has probably been a ferry across the Tamar between East Stonehouse and West Stonehouse (now known as Cremyll) since Saxon times. West Stonehouse and much of the Maker peninsula was part of Devon from then until 1844, and a marker in the wall of a house in Cawsand called 'Devon–Corn' still shows where the boundary lay.

The right to run a ferry here was granted to the Durnford family by the local lord of the Manor, and passed to the Edgcumbes when Sir Piers Edgcumbe of Cotehele married Joan Durnford in 1493. The Edgcumbe family retained the rights to the Cremyll ferry until 1946, and it is now managed jointly by Plymouth and Cornwall councils. The ferry service is provided by Plymouth Boat Trips.

As the ferryboat was rowed with sweeps, the ferrymen naturally chose the shortest passage, from the sheltered north side of Devil's Point across to a suitable landing place at Wilderness Point (near to where the Tudor battery stands). The tide runs strongly here, with the waters of the Tamar, Tavy and Lynher rivers supplementing the estuarial saltwater on the ebb tide. Considerable skill is needed to row across the Narrows when the tide is running, as strong eddies and whirlpools can pull you in a direction you hadn't bargained for (as the writer can testify).

The ferry was required to handle horses and even carts, which would be towed or paddled across on a barge or 'horse boat', although some of the rowing boats were substantial enough to enable horses to be carried as well as people. A cast iron winch which was used to haul the horse boats up the beach still stands on the quay at Cremyll.

In 1791 a ferry service started from 'New Passage' across to Torpoint, where a new turnpike had been built. Traffic by ferry from Devil's Point across the river dwindled, and it appears that at some stage the ferry may have run from Mutton Cove, adjacent to South Yard, as a map of 1820 shows this as the route of the Cremyll ferry. Construction of Clarence Wharf and the Royal William Yard from 1824 stimulated the development of Stonehouse along Durnford Street, and also necessitated constructing a new paved slipway or 'hard' (known as Admiral's Hard) for the ferry in Stonehouse Pool. From Admiral's Hard the ferryboat ran to a quay adjacent to the Edgcumbe Arms in Cremyll. Despite the greatly increased distance, rowing boats continued to be used until 1885, when the first steam-powered ferries were introduced. They were fitted with diesel engines in 1945.

The Cremyll ferry continues to provide Plymothians with easy access to the gardens, woods and hills of Mount Edgcumbe Park. In the summer months it is heavily used, although parking facilities within walking distance of Admiral's Hard are minimal, and there is no park-and-ride service provided.

71. MOUNT EDGCUMBE PARK AND FOLLY

Magnificent views of the Sound and across Plymouth to Dartmoor

The casual visitor to the city might be excused for thinking that Plymouth is not much of a place. Yes, the Barbican is pretty enough, but for many people the centre lacks character, and unless you walk up to the Hoe you might not even realise that it stands on the edge of the sea. But cross over the Tamar into Cornwall and walk up to the Folly in Mount Edgcumbe Park, and you see what a magnificent position Plymouth occupies – backed by the purple slopes of Dartmoor and standing at the inner end of one of the fine st natural harbours in the world.

Standing here, there's always something of interest to see: perhaps a warship being escorted around Drake's Island into the narrow channel at the mouth of the Tamar, or fleets of colourful dinghies jostling each other as they race around the buoys, or a powerboat carving a slice across the sheltered waters below Jennycliff.

Mount Edgcumbe Park was laid out in the mid-eighteenth century, when the fashion was for English landscape gardens as popularised by Capability Brown, featuring lakes, sweeping lawns backed by groves of trees, classical temples, picturesque ruins and ornamental bridges, and specimen trees like cedars and Monterey pines. Landscape gardens were designed to create an idyllic pastoral landscape like those pictured in Renaissance art, featuring idealised vistas of hilly wooded Arcadian countryside. All those features can be found here.

The Folly stands on a slight knoll on the lower slopes of Maker Heights, and can be seen from the Hoe and much of the seafront. It was built in 1747 on the site of a navigation obelisk and later incorporated stone from St Lawrence's Chapel, which stood beside the old ferry passage near Devil's Point.

This Grade 1 listed park boasts a stately Giant Redwood (Sequoia) and the National Camellia Collection, as well a herd of deer which can often be seen grazing the downs on Maker Heights. Between Cremyll and the Folly lie the formal gardens laid out in the late 1700s, including an Italian Garden with the magnificent Orangery of 1760 (serving teas and restaurant food), a French Garden, and a Grotto containing the poignant grave-stones of Edgcumbe family pets, and an English Garden, with formal rose beds and lawns, summerhouses and some fine old cork trees. Recent additions include a New Zealand Garden and an American Garden, and the Jubilee Garden opened in 2002 to celebrate the Queen's Golden Jubilee.

From the formal gardens the path along the cliff to the Folly takes you past one of the Tudor forts, and Barn Pool, where Darwin set sail in HMS *Beagle* in 1831, and where landing craft were loaded before D-Day.

Mount Edgcumbe Country Park and formal gardens are open all year round and admission is free.

PLYMOUTH'S RARE FLORA AND FAUNA

The Plymouth area is home to many rare plant species and marine creatures.

The sea off Plymouth is one of the few places you can see red bandfish, eel-like creatures with large eyes and a big mouth which can grow up to a metre long. Spiny and short-snouted (left) seahorses are found in the Sound. It is also one of the rare places where you can see fan shells, fragile bivalves like mussels.

The pink sea fan is one of the UK's most spectacular soft corals. There are colonies in Lyme Bay which are protected from fishing, yet they can also be found a couple of miles off the Plymouth coast.

The pink flowered bladder campion called Plymouth Campion (Silene vulgaris ssp. vulgaris) has been found on Plymouth Hoe since 1921. It is native to the Mediterranean, and no one knows how it arrived here.

There is also the Plymouth Thistle (Carduus pycnocephalus), which is found in the Mediterranean, North Africa, Eastern Europe and even India. In Australia and New Zealand it is classed as a noxious weed. It is sometimes confused with the slender thistle, which has fewer spiny stems and smaller flower clusters. Plymouth Thistle can carry as many as ten, and the flowers have stalks. The Plymouth Thistle is not found elsewhere in the British Isles.

The Plymouth Strawberry (Fragaria vesca var. muricata) is only found in the damp deciduous woodlands of Plymouth. It is one of the strangest of Plymouth's subspecies, a bit like an ordinary wild strawberry but with green leafy flowers instead of white. Also it is not nearly so pleasant to eat, as the fruits are covered in green spines.

Finally, there is the Plymouth Pear (Pyrus cordata), so

called because Plymouth is the place where it was first identified in 1870. It grows in hedgerows or at the edge of woods. It is one of the rarest trees in the UK and indeed only a handful of them have been found naturally occurring in the whole world. It is protected under the Wildlife & Countryside Act, and is one of the 39,000 species of plants whose seeds have been deposited at Kew's Millennium Seed Bank.

Andrew Young from the Plymouth Tree Partnership describes the Plymouth Pear as "a bit of a mystery. They were first found on the outskirts of Plymouth and appear in only a few hedgerows in Devon and Cornwall. But they're also found in Brittany and in Northern Spain and that makes people think they were the last tree to come to Britain after the last Ice Age when the ice melted and the English Channel was formed".

Plymouth Pear trees can grow to about 35 feet, rather larger than the ordinary pear tree. The blossom is pale cream with some pink, which looks good but smells awful – it has been compared to rotting scampi, soiled sheets or wet carpets, and tends to attract flies. The fruit resembles a crab apple, and is inedible.

Most of its seeds are infertile as it lacks genetic diversity, the flowers being hermaphrodite. Conservation work is based on trying to increase that genetic spread, and it is hoped that some mutations will take place with the cultivated stock which will allow them to breed more successfully.

Stoke Damerel

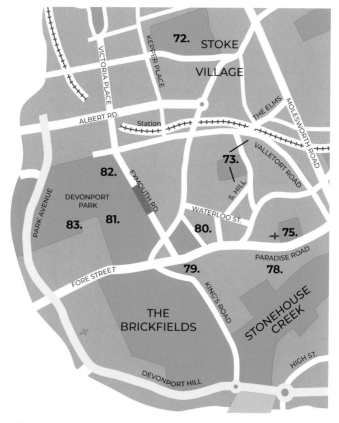

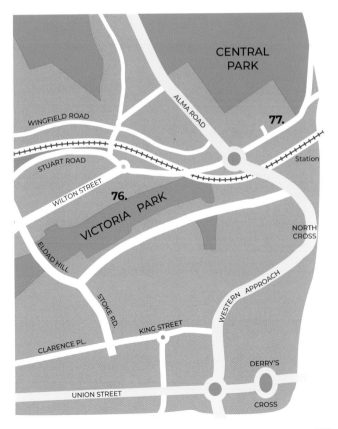

72. MOUNT PLEASANT REDOUBT, STOKE

18th century blockhouse with 360° view over Plymouth

The late eighteenth and early nineteenth centuries were years of war with France as well as America and Spain. By then 'Dock' had become one of Britain's main naval bases, enclosed within its own defensive fortification known as the Lines. But overlooking the Dock Lines was Mount Pleasant, half a mile to the north-east and 230 feet above sea level.

A shallow ditch and earth rampart had been built here in the 1750s, but the event which precipitated the fortification of the site was the Franco-Spanish attempt to invade England in 1779. The combined fleet of 66 enemy ships lay at anchor in Cawsand Bay for several days, while the British Channel Fleet was away patrolling off the Scillies. Fortunately disease and indecisiveness caused the invasion to be abandoned, and the fleet was driven west by gales.

Improvements to English fortifications along the south coast were hastily put in hand. In Plymouth it was decided to fortify Mount Pleasant in order to prevent an enemy from mounting siege guns there, overlooking the Lines. A thousand local miners were conscripted to build the redoubt and carry out other works around Dock which the local military engineer, Colonel Dixon, had recommended, and it was completed in three months in early 1780.

Mount Pleasant Redoubt is about 140 feet square, with ramparts of earth revetted with brick and surrounded by a ditch. The outer face of the ramparts would have had sharpened wooden stakes embedded into it. The single entrance on the south side was protected by a drawbridge. The fort had eleven 18-pounder guns mounted on the north and east ramparts, the position of which can still be seen. In the middle of the redoubt was a two-storey blockhouse which was connected by an underground passage to a magazine beneath the south western rampart.

The Battle of Waterloo in 1815 brought to an end centuries of war with France dating back to the Norman invasion of 1066, and happily the two countries have not fought each other since. Mount Pleasant Redoubt was mothballed, and played no part in the ring of 'Palmerston forts' built in the 1860s around Plymouth and Devonport. The redoubt last saw active service in the Second World War when an anti-aircraft battery was mounted here, together with a barrage balloon tethered to what remained of the old blockhouse.

After the war the remains of the blockhouse were removed and the site was opened as a public park. It is a popular place for dog-walkers, and includes a children's playground and exercise equipment.

The views are splendid on a clear day – the tors and heather-clad slopes of Dartmoor to the north, to the west the Dockyard and the hills of Cornwall down as far as Caradon, to the south the Sound, and to the east the City Centre. An engraved disc shows the compass points and helps identify the main landmarks.

73. BLITZ DAMAGE, STOKE DAMEREL

Surviving evidence of the Blitz of 1940–41

The German invasion of France in 1940 gave the Luftwaffe access to Plymouth and its dockyard, and the first bombs fell in Swilly Road, Keyham (now North Prospect Road) on 6 July 1940 – three bombs dropped, three people died and three houses were destroyed. A pattern of small raids continued, seemingly targeting the dockyard, the railway station and gas and electric plants, but more often than not destroying nearby houses and shops.

The city was unprepared. As the Blitz intensified, thousands would trek out into the country each night, sleeping in village halls, in the homes of villagers, in tents and under hedges, returning to the city the next day to work. High-explosive bombs started to be used, and the raids increased in frequency and ferocity.

On 20 March 1941 the King and Queen visited the city to help boost morale. The Royal Train was still on its way back to London when a devastating raid on the city centre by around 125 bombers heralded the start of the most intense period of destruction, and an equally heavy raid took place the following night. In the space of those two nights the shopping centre was obliterated. The raids continued throughout 1941, with around 200,000 incendiary bombs and 6,500 high explosive bombs being dropped. From 1942 the raids gradually petered out, and the last bombs fell on 30 April 1944.

By then Plymouth had suffered 59 enemy air attacks. 1,174 civilians had been killed and 1,092 seriously injured; nearly 5,000 buildings had been destroyed, and about 71,000 damaged. Churches, schools, hospitals, factories and shops – the devastation seems unimaginable to us. What would you have done if you had emerged wearily from a shelter in the early hours of the morning to find your home destroyed, and the remains of your possessions scattered across the street? One morning after a raid, the Plymouth MP Nancy Astor came across a young woman standing speechless beside a heap of rubble and timber which until last night had been her home. Now it was gone, and so were her baby, her mother and grandmother. Lady Astor stood with her arm around her until she was able to move. For the size of its population and the intensity and scale of the bombing, Plymouth was the worst-hit city in the country.

That was 80 years ago. But the scars still remain. In April 1941 high-explosive bombs fell on or near the bridge carrying Valletort Road over the rail access to the GWR's Devonport Goods Depot, leaving these shrapnel holes in the bridge girders on the south side.

Many Plymouth terraces have gaps where houses were destroyed and new houses built. On 21 March 1941 bombs destroyed two of a terrace of late Georgian houses in nearby South Hill, and the 1960s-style houses which replaced them are typical of the post-war infill. No.16, the end terrace house on the opposite side, is no more, and only the gap in the street numbers and the tell-tale buttress formed of part of the front wall show where once it stood.

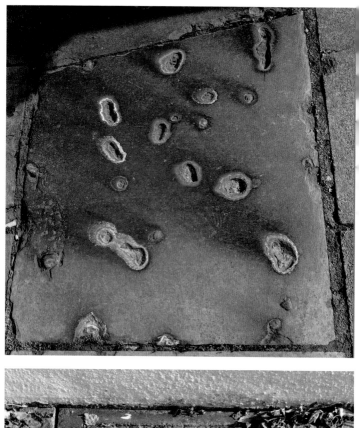

74. PAVEMENT MARKINGS, STOKE DAMEREL

The interesting things you find beneath your feet

There is often much to see simply by looking down at the pavement. In South Hill, see if you can find the two surviving cast-iron lids giving access to the coal holes beneath, marked 'Morris Devonport'. They are a rare survival and remind us that in former times there were foundries and ironworks in most towns, each with their own distinctive markings. Plymouth had several.

In adjoining Waterloo Street are a number of paving slabs on the north side showing the marks of incendiaries dropped during the Second World War. Incendiary bombs contained thermite, a mixture of metal powder and metal oxide, typically aluminium or magnesium with iron oxide. When these combined on impact, the chemical reaction produced a brief burst of extreme heat (around 2,500 degrees). Petrol was used in incendiaries when metals became in short supply. The picture opposite shows the result of an incendiary bomb falling nearby, showering the area with burning metal hot enough to bore into stone. Some of the metal remains embedded in the holes, and the streaking resulting from the flow of burning material down the slope of the pavement can still be clearly seen.

There are also examples of kerbstone marks in Waterloo Street, as in the picture below. There are competing theories as to what they signify. It may be that they indicate stones which were cut so as to fit the curved pavement edge on a street corner. The stone on the left bears the symbols +++. But what of the initials NT on the adjoining stone? An analysis of kerb symbols in London and Glasgow suggested that they were cut by the mason or gang of masons responsible for laying kerbstones and cobbles, to show how much work they had done that day, as masons were paid according to the amount of stones they cut.

But the truth is that no one knows.

75. STOKE DAMEREL CHURCHYARD

A graveyard's lurid history

The churchyard at Stoke Damerel seems peaceful enough now. The gravestones have been removed leaving pleasant lawns, and squirrels scamper around the fine old trees in the lower park. Near the north door of the church is the railed-off grave of Captain Tobias Furneaux of Swilly, who sailed with Captain Cook and was one of the first people to circumnavigate the world in both directions. But the churchyard's past is not so placid.

In 1788 a dockyard clerk named Philip Smith was killed there by a blow to the head. Suspicion fell on John Richards, a violent and disreputable character who had been sacked from the dockyard and appeared to blame Smith for it. He had been seen lurking near the churchyard with an accomplice. They were tried for murder at Exeter Assizes where they were convicted and sentenced to be hanged, with their bodies to be hung in iron cages near to the scene of their crime until they had rotted away.

A double gibbet was erected beside the road at the edge of Stonehouse Creek near the churchyard, about where Devonport High School's sports hall now stands (before the creek was drained and filled, there was a muddy tidal estuary from Stonehouse Bridge as far as Pennycomequick). It is said that it took seven years for the gruesome remains to rot away. It was not until nearly 40 years later that the gibbet finally collapsed into the ooze. But it's an ill wind that blows nobody any good, and a carpenter retrieved pieces of the timber for making snuff boxes, which apparently sold well.

Thomas Goslin and his wife Louisa were professional 'resurrectionists' or body-snatchers, who had established a lucrative trade supplying corpses to London medical schools. One of his first clients was Sir Astley Cooper of Guy's Hospital, a very eminent surgeon of the early 1800s. In law, a corpse belonged to no one and the penalties for taking one were relatively light, while the price paid by anatomists for a fresh one was substantial. The very best techniques were employed – using wooden shovels to mask the noise, and digging tunnels along a line of graves to remove several bodies without disturbing the surface.

The Goslins were caught grave robbing several times, but appear to have regarded that as an inevitable business risk. They practised in London, Maidstone, Manchester, Great Yarmouth and Colchester, before moving to what is now Wilton Street in Stoke Damerel in 1830. It was there that they made their fatal mistake. For while taking a body was a mere misdemeanour, taking the grave-clothes was theft, punishable by hanging or transportation. An astute police officer found out what they were up to and lay in wait in the churchyard the night after an interment. The Goslins and their two accomplices were caught, and a search of their home revealed not only bodies and piles of teeth but a heap of grave-clothes too. They were transported to a convict colony in Tasmania and never returned to England.

76. PROPRIETARY LIBRARY, OFF WILTON STREET

Among the earliest subscription libraries, with over 20,000 books

The oldest lending library in Britain is Chetham's, which opened in Manchester in 1653, but libraries only became more numerous a century or more later when secular literature and novels started to be popular. Most of them were subscription libraries, where subscribers would pay an annual fee for membership, and the library would use this income to expand its collection of books.

They were set up by local people with the aim of establishing a permanent collection of books and reading materials. Committees elected by the subscribers would choose books for the collection, usually ones of general interest which would have a broad appeal. Some of these libraries were 'proprietary' libraries which required subscribers to invest in shares as well as paying an annual fee.

The Plymouth Proprietary Library was founded in 1810, making it among the oldest surviving in the country, and claims to be "home to more than 20,000 books, from some of the oldest and rarest in Devon right through to modern bestselling novels". It has a huge fiction section, based in the Long Room, including a specialist crime section. Up to 30 new titles are added every two months.

The library also has a large biography section with letters and diaries, a room dedicated to local history books including the Windham Collection of Royal Naval historical papers, and a significant poetry collection, including 1,000 poetry books bequeathed by the Devon poet Simon Curtis. It also contains some very rare books such as a unique Catholic Prayer-book dating from 1716. The Cottonian Collection, presented to the library in 1853 by William Cotton, is currently housed in Plymouth Museum and administered jointly by Plymouth City Council and Plymouth Proprietary Library.

The Proprietary Library was founded two years before the Plymouth Institution (now called Plymouth Athenaeum), a society dedicated to the promotion of learning in the fields of science, technology, literature and art, with lectures by knowledgeable people and an extensive library of its own. Both institutions were housed in fine Doric-style buildings at Derry's Cross, designed by John Foulston. The Proprietary Library building included a magnificent reading room with shelves on two floors surmounted by a domed lantern. Sadly, both were destroyed by enemy action in 1941, and the library lost most of its collection. But its members found another building and began the task of restocking it even as the war continued.

While the Athenaeum was rebuilt in 1960s style on its original site, including a small theatre with a revolving stage, the Proprietary Library moved to North Hill, where it remained until it moved recently to part of St Barnabas' Church, below Wilton Street.

77. OLD DEVONPORT PRISON, PENNYCOMEQUICK

Surviving Warden's house and Gatehouse of old model prison

In 1835 the Borough of Devonport was enlarged to include Stoke Damerel parish, extending it east right up to what is now Central Park.

Talks had taken place in the 1840s between the borough councils of Devonport and Plymouth about having a joint prison, but no agreement could be reached. Plymouth therefore built its own prison at Greenbank in 1851 (part of the building remains, next to Aldi) and the 'Devonport Borough Gaol & House of Correction' was completed two months later. It stood in what is now Central Park Avenue but was then known as Cemetery Road, Pennycomequick.

The architect was James Piers St Aubyn, a prominent church architect whose style was firmly in the Gothic revival mainstream of his time. The prison itself was typical of many Victorian gaols, with a central ventilation tower and small arched windows preventing inmates from seeing much except the sky, but the Warden's house and ornamental gatehouse were in the domestic Gothic style of the fourteenth century.

The prison was built to take 70 inmates, with 44 cells for men, 12 for women and 14 for debtors. The Warden and prison officials took the enlightened view that a prison should be a place for rehabilitating offenders so that they could become useful citizens, and not merely a place of punishment. It appears that they were supported in this by the local magistrates, who were sparing in the use of hard labour as a punishment.

It was held up as a model of economy by the Prison Inspectors, as the cost of upkeep was just £29 a year for each inmate, half the cost of any other prison. A dietary table for the prison shows that inmates were given carefully measured meals based on the length of their sentence: inmates serving a week or less were only given bread for breakfast, supper and dinner, with 'Indian meal' or potatoes on weekdays. Gruel, suet pudding, soup and cheese were added in increasing amounts according to the length of the sentence.

There was a separate diet for those on hard labour, but it was considered that the cost of this in relation to the value of the labour undertaken made it uneconomical.

However, an inspection by naval officials of the provisions for convicted sailors found a general lack of discipline not in keeping with naval standards. "Prisoners were seen chatting amiably with the guards and leaving their meagre cells littered and unkempt". There was also criticism of the lack of proper bedding.

The Prisons Act of 1877 brought all local prisons under government control, and Devonport was closed in 1878 after only 27 years' use. The prison was later demolished apart from the Warden's house and Gateway, and a matching wing was later added on the east side. They remain in use as private houses.

78. DEVONPORT HIGH SCHOOL FOR BOYS

Former military hospital associated with the strange case of Dr James Barry

This fine building with its magnificent colonnade, said to be the longest in Europe, was established in 1797 as Stoke Military Hospital. Like the Royal Naval Hospital on the opposite side of Stonehouse Creek, it was constructed on hygienic principles in the pavilion style, with separate blocks dealing with different medical conditions to minimise the risk of cross-infection. French prisoners of war, who were accommodated in hulks in the Hamoaze, were drafted in to assist with the work. The hospital treated sick and injured soldiers from Napoleonic times until after the Second World War when it was decommissioned, and it has been occupied by Devonport High School for Boys since 1945.

Margaret Bulkley was born in Cork in about 1789. It is thought that she gave birth to a daughter after being raped in childhood, although the baby was passed off as her sister. She was an intelligent young woman who wished to practice as a surgeon, a profession which in those days was restricted to men. With the assistance of family friends she was admitted to Edinburgh Medical School as a boy, James Barry, a change of gender which was retained all her life. Barry qualified as a surgeon in 1813 and joined the Army Medical Corps, serving at Stoke Military Hospital until 1816 when he was posted to Cape Town.

There he proved to be an excellent surgeon, rapidly becoming the Colonial Medical Inspector and later Surgeon to the South African Forces. He was responsible for effecting improvements to sanitation and water supply, and improving living conditions for the marginalised – slaves, prisoners, lepers and the mentally ill. He also performed the first successful Caesarean section in Africa. Later postings included the West Indies, Malta, Corfu and Canada, where he was promoted to the medical equivalent of Brigadier General.

Throughout his career he insisted on improvements to sanitation, diet and the treatment of the poor and needy, but his heavy handedness and lack of tact often aroused anger and opposition, on one occasion provoking a duel in which he got the better of his opponent. On an informal visit to Scutari Hospital during the Crimean War in the 1850s he had a fierce argument with Florence Nightingale, who wrote that he berated her and "behaved like a brute ... I should say that [Barry] was the most hardened creature I ever met".

Contemporary accounts of Dr Barry commented on his 'effeminacy' and his rather high voice, but while his argumentative nature and fierce temper were regretted, he was praised for his professional skill and good bedside manner. Photographs of him explain why he had no difficulty passing as a man. He never allowed anyone to examine him or see him dressing, and directed that after his death his body should be buried in the bed-sheets "without further inspection". Unfortunately this instruction was not observed by the woman who prepared his body for burial, who told the press of his true nature. He is buried in Kensal Green Cemetery under the name James Barry.

79. FORMER DEVONPORT KING'S ROAD STATION

Once Plymouth's finest railway station, now City College

M ost of Britain's railway system was built over the space of only 40 years or so in the mid nineteenth century by separate companies in competition with each other, providing a classic illustration of both the strengths and weaknesses of the capitalist system. The company that provided the fastest journey or cheapest route between major cities could expect the most custom, but as a result there was a lot of unnecessary duplication, and rationalisation became inevitable with the post-war growth of motor traffic.

It had long been the ambition of the London & South Western Railway (LSWR) to break the monopoly which the Great Western enjoyed in Devon and Cornwall. The LSWR had reached Exeter in 1860, and steadily continued west towards Plymouth around the north of Dartmoor via Okehampton. In 1874 it finally reached Lydford, where it obtained running rights over the Great Western's single-track branch from Plymouth to Launceston via Tavistock. It took four years for the GWR to convert the broad gauge track to mixed gauge, so it was not until 1876 that the first train from London Waterloo arrived at the LSWR's terminus at Devonport King's Road. It was met with much celebration and the expectation of cheaper fares as the two companies competed for traffic.

Devonport King's Road was a fine stone-built station with a steel-and-glass overall roof, very much more impressive than the GWR's ramshackle wooden station at North Road or its rather plain Millbay terminus. It stood on the site now occupied by City College, although only the arched retaining wall alongside Paradise Road and the station approach roads remain.

Sharing the single-track route between Marsh Mills and Lydford with GWR branch trains caused considerable inconvenience and delay, and it became clear that an independent route to Plymouth would have to be built. In 1883 the Plymouth, Devonport & South Western Junction Railway was formed to build a line from Devonport King's Road to Bere Alston, Tavistock and Lydford. This proved to be one of the most expensive lines, mile for mile, ever built, as the track had to be shoe-horned around late nineteenth century housing developments, and scarcely more than a few miles followed the natural contours of the land. There were many stone-built viaducts, the long girder bridge over the mouth of the Tavy and several tunnels, and much of the line ran in deep cuttings or high embankments. Despite this, the line was completed in only three years, opening in 1890.

Just west of City College there is a wooden door leading into a nature reserve. At the far end of this, beyond the bridge where London-bound trains passed under Paradise Road, is the mouth of a tunnel. This took trains deep under Devonport Park, snatching a breath in a short cutting beside Exmouth Road before plunging beneath the GWR's tunnel at Devonport station and continuing under Victoria Place to emerge high above Ford Valley onto a stone viaduct (now no more).

80. ALBEMARLE VILLAS

A fine row of houses dating from the 1820s, where Guy Burgess was born

One of the finest group of houses in Plymouth is Albemarle Villas, designed by John Foulston in the 1820s, and still looking across an open field (though now used by dog walkers and no longer grazed by sheep). Many of the villas retain their delightful wrought iron balconies in the Regency style and other period features.

Foulston was a London architect who was appointed Plymouth's Town Architect in 1810 after winning a competition to design a new hotel and theatre. His Royal Hotel, Theatre and Assembly Rooms at Derry's Clock in the Greek Revival style was an elegant ornament in the heart of the city. Built in stone, it was the first building to incorporate cast and wrought iron in its structure. Incredibly, the theatre was demolished in the 1930s in a blatant case of civic vandalism, and replaced with the Odeon-style cinema which still stands (now unused).

Foulston did much to enhance the architecture of Plymouth and had grand plans for rebuilding the central area. He was responsible for the design of Union Street, laid out between 1812 and 1820 to connect the Three Towns of Plymouth, East Stonehouse and Devonport, and also designed the grand villas at Penlee Gardens. He built the grand town centre of Devonport at Ker Street, as we shall see. However posterity has not dealt kindly with his legacy, and much of what remains has been altered beyond recognition. Some of it disappeared in the Blitz or the post-war reconstruction.

Perhaps the most notorious inhabitant of Albemarle Villas was the spy Guy Burgess, who was born at No 2 in 1911, the oldest son of a Royal Naval officer. While at Cambridge University in 1930 he joined the Communist Party, and was introduced to Arnold Deutsch, a Soviet spy. He went to Moscow in 1934 and started to recruit other like-minded students, Anthony Blunt, Donald Maclean, Kim Philby and John Cairncross. Like them, Burgess was a heavy drinker and openly gay. Despite his membership of the Communist Party he worked variously in MI6, the BBC and the Foreign Office in the 1930s and 40s without apparently arousing suspicion, continuing to pass information to the USSR.

After the war it appears his drunkenness became problematic. He was given a post in the Washington Embassy but was sent back to the UK after being caught speeding three times in Virginia.

In 1951, the CIA became suspicious of Maclean, and Philby, who was the head of MI6 in Washington, got to hear of it. It seemed that the net had finally begun to close around the Cambridge Five. Fearing arrest, Burgess and Maclean defected to the USSR, and Philby joined them in 1963. But the Soviet state proved not to be the paradise they imagined. Burgess developed a nostalgic longing for all things English, and suffered a deep depression which he relieved with alcohol. He died in 1963 when only 52.

81. DEVONPORT PARK

The People's Park, recently revived with Heritage Lottery funding

Plymouth has many parks and open spaces, and the oldest of these is Devonport Park, a Grade II registered historic park which was established in the 1850s. The green belt surrounding the defensive Lines encircling Devonport's barracks, which had been under military control and used for training exercises, became somewhere for ladies to stroll beneath their parasols, and gentlemen in straw hats to sit in deckchairs listening to the band playing in the bandstand.

During the Second World War the park came under military control again in preparation for D-Day. Concrete roads were made so that lines of Sherman tanks, DUKWs and other military hardware could be assembled beneath the trees ready for the signal to head for the embarkation points.

Like most public spaces, Devonport Park saw a slow decline towards the end of the twentieth century, as the paths and planted areas deteriorated and fewer and fewer people used it. The park's bandstand was demolished in the 1950s as it was no longer safe, and the two ornamental fountains dating from the late nineteenth century had long ceased to function. Happily, the park was selected for funding by English Heritage as part of the millennial regeneration scheme, and £3.3 million was awarded to Plymouth City Council by the Heritage Lottery (although the total cost of restoration eventually exceeded £5 million).

Between 2008 and 2011 the many paths were relaid, a play activity area for children of different ages was made, and a new pavilion built in the middle of the park with a café, community room and sports facilities. The fountains were brought back into use, a new bandstand was built, and the unusual Swiss style park-keeper's lodge (the Lower Lodge) was rescued from dereliction. Many areas have been replanted.

Of particular interest is the 'Doris Gun' memorial near the central pavilion, which was erected following the end of the Boer War of 1899 to 1902 to commemorate the men of the cruiser HMS *Doris*, who took part in two shore actions involving Royal Marines supported by naval seamen. Two of HMS *Doris*' 4.7" guns were removed from the ship, mounted on improvised carriages and manhandled hundreds of miles across the veldt, in a move which enabled the British to match the firepower of the Boers in the Battle of Paardeberg and helped to turn the tide of the war.

The Doris Gun is a genuine 'pom-pom' captured from the Boers, a 37 mm Maxim-Nordenfelt quick-firing gun mounted on a standard artillery carriage. This was a large calibre, water-cooled recoil-loaded weapon firing explosive rounds from a cartridge belt at 450 rounds a minute, and was the first true auto-cannon. The trigger-guard and handgrip are evident, strangely resembling those on an ordinary revolver, and the screw mechanism to correct the elevation can be clearly seen.

82. SOAPBOX THEATRE, DEVONPORT PARK

Former WWII Gas Cleansing unit, now an enterprising children's theatre

"I have to tell you now that no such undertaking has been received, and consequently this country is at war with Germany". Chamberlain's measured but chilling words in his radio broadcast of 3 September 1939 following the German invasion of Poland prompted immediate preparations for enemy action. Besides building air-raid shelters and organising wardens to marshal people towards them and enforce the blackout regulations, it was thought necessary to counter the threat of gas or chemical weapons being dropped on civilian populations. The horrors of the mustard gas attacks on soldiers in the First World War was still fresh in people's minds.

Gas masks were issued to civilians – horrible, dehumanising things that smelt of rubber. Gas Cleansing Centres were set up to treat those suffering from poison gas. One of these, a brick structure looking like a large air-raid shelter, is in Devonport Park.

Fortunately gas and chemical weapons were never used, although by the end of the war Nazi Germany had produced some 12,000 tons of deadly sarin gas, enough to kill millions. Britain also manufactured such weapons and made no secret of doing so, probably as a warning that if the Germans used such weapons against us we would retaliate in kind. Churchill was prepared to use chemical weapons, but only if the enemy unleashed them first. In February 1943, when it was discovered that the Germans were considering using gas against the Russians in the Donets Basin, Churchill wrote to his Chiefs of Staffs Committee: "In the event of the Germans using gas on the Russians ... we shall retaliate by drenching the German cities with gas on the largest possible scale".

While this may explain why it was never used in Britain, it may seem strange that Hitler never authorised its use against other countries, given the regular use of poison gas in the extermination camps. Hitler resisted the urgings of senior Nazis and military officers to use it against the USSR as the conflict on the eastern front became a war of attrition which Germany was steadily losing. But it appears that Hitler himself suffered from poison gas while he was serving in the trenches during the First World War, and it may be that he had no wish to encounter it again.

After the war the building escaped demolition, and was used for a time as a model railway clubhouse. It then remained empty until 2014 when it was refurbished and opened as Stiltskin's Soapbox Children's Theatre. As well as staging regular plays and pantomimes suitable for children, the Soapbox Theatre is a 'community space' where children and their families can come together to take part in cultural projects such as drama, dance and art workshops, holiday clubs and festivals.

83. THE DEVONPORT LINES

Surviving section of the defensive walls surrounding Devonport

Although Sutton Harbour had long been a base for warships, until the late 1600s the only dockyard for building major warships or carrying out extensive repairs was at Portsmouth. The ending of the Dutch wars following the Glorious Revolution of 1688, which brought the Dutchman William of Orange and his wife Mary Stuart to the throne, shifted the threat from the Low Countries to France and the Western Approaches. Cherbourg had been fortified by the great French military engineer Vauban in the 1680s, and a great dockyard was being built at Brest. Building a naval dockyard at Plymouth became a priority. After considering and rejecting Turnchapel as a possible site (although warships were later built here), in 1691 work began on building a yard for repairing warships on the Hamoaze just north of Froward Point, which juts out near where the Covered Slip is now.

Dock (as Devonport was originally called) steadily expanded northwards, and along with the additional dockyard facilities came houses and shops to cater for the growing numbers employed there. By 1733 Plymouth Dock had some 3,000 inhabitants, although it was not until later that any schools were built, and the nearest church was at Stoke Damerel. But beer and whores were easy to obtain, and it was known as a hard-living place where workmen supplemented their meagre pay by pilfering dockyard stores.

Even as it grew, Dock remained a military town, built to service the warships of the Royal Navy and the garrisons stationed there. A defensive ring around it was made in 1757 during the War of Austrian Succession although it was little more than a shallow ditch and earth rampart. It was not until 1810, when the wars with France were almost over, that the Dock Lines (as they were called) became massive ramparts faced with stone and a deep ditch. The work ended with the defeat of Napoleon at the Battle of Waterloo in 1815, and the Lines were not completed until the 1850s.

Parts of the Lines remain discernible, although most of the wall has disappeared. The most impressive surviving stretch is at Devonport Park near the Doris gun. The walls would have appeared much higher than they do now because the ditch has been filled in.

This section may have survived because it also served as a reservoir for the Devonport Leat which brought a reliable source of clean water from Dartmoor to Devonport. The Devonport Leat was built in the 1790s and originally ended in various piped conduits in the town, but at some stage a large reservoir was made outside the Lines, using the stone walls of the ramparts for three sides and with a smaller wall on the north side to contain the water. It was known as the Granby Reservoir since Granby Barracks lay the other side of the wall.

Some remains of the Lines can also be seen at Devonport Hill, including the defensive ditch and the remains of a drawbridge.

Devonport and Keyham

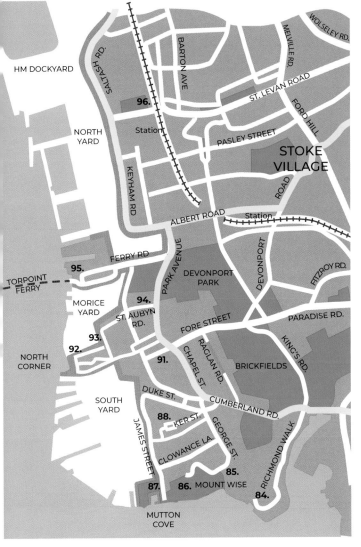

84. DEVONPORT'S UNDERGROUND HQ

Plymouth's nuclear bunker and WWII command centre

This small blast-proof door in the wall alongside Richmond Walk below the Scott Memorial is all that alerts us to a hidden place which for many years was top secret.

By 1937 it was becoming clear to the military chiefs that Europe was once again heading for conflict. Plans were made to build underground bunkers capable of withstanding a direct hit by a 500lb bomb, to house the area commanders of the Navy, Army and RAF in the event of war. One of these was at Mount Wise, and the area chosen was the dry ditch originally forming part of the Dockyard Lines in the grounds of Admiralty House. This fine house (recently converted for private occupation) was built to house the Governor of the Dockyard, but for many years was the home of the Flag Officer, Plymouth.

The bunker was complete and fully operational by 1941. In 1942, with the threat of invasion receding and planning for D-Day in progress, more space to accommodate US military command personnel became necessary, and an extension (including a major communications hub) was built beneath the lawns of Admiralty House. At the heart of the bunker was the Joint Operations Room, a layout familiar from many war films, with WAAFs moving flags around the central table with their 'billiard cues' and officers gazing down on developments from three glass-fronted galleries.

The main bunker remained in daily use after the Second World War, providing command facilities for NATO operations in the Eastern Atlantic and for intelligence and maritime surveillance. In the mid 1980s and early 1990s the facility was comprehensively upgraded to make it suitable for use in the event of nuclear war, although it was never capable of withstanding a direct hit. The old plotting maps were replaced with computers and improved air conditioning and air filtration units were installed. The bunker remained in operational use until 2004, and as late as 2003 the Devonport Communications Centre was housed there.

The main entrance to the Mount Wise complex is the ramp from Richmond Walk alongside Stonehouse Creek leading up to a stone arch, through which is what appears to be just one of the many nineteenth century fortifications around Plymouth. In the small courtyard behind there is a guardroom, and beyond that an airlock leading into the lower floor of the bunker. The bunker itself is a complex of rooms and corridors on two levels including a telephone exchange and radio communications room.

Following decommissioning in 2004 it was mothballed, with only the communications plant remaining in use. The sale of the Mount Wise site by the MOD in 2014 for private development saw various uses proposed for the bunker, but currently its future remains uncertain.

85. SCOTT MONUMENT, MOUNT WISE

Remembering Scott of the Antarctic, Britain's poignant hero

" Had we lived, I should have had a tale to tell of the hardihood, endurance and courage of my companions which would have stirred the heart of every Englishman. These rough notes and our dead bodies must tell the tale".

This passage from the final diary entry which Captain Scott made, while he and two colleagues lay in a small tent, whipped by freezing winds and waiting to die, surrounds the monument erected to his memory. Perhaps as much as anything else, these extraordinarily poignant words ensured his place as the quintessential British hero – carrying on valiantly and against all the odds to achieve a noble and heroic failure.

Robert Falcon Scott was born in 1868 at Outlands House, which stood in substantial grounds near Milehouse crossroads and St Bartholomew's Church. It was demolished following major damage during the Second World War. Scott served as an officer in the Royal Navy, having reached the rank of Commander when he was appointed to lead the British Antarctic Survey of 1901-1904, a scientific expedition to discover more about the flora, fauna and geology of the continent. This expedition, which also included the young Ernest Shackleton, was successful in achieving a number of important goals, as well as providing valuable experience of survival in extreme weather conditions. On his return, Scott was feted as a hero and awarded many medals and honours, and was promoted to the rank of Captain.

After a year or so on the lecture circuit he returned to the Royal Navy, commanding the battleship HMS *Albemarle*. In 1908 he married, and their son Peter Scott (the well-known naturalist who founded the World Wildlife Fund) was born a year later.

The ill-fated *Terra Nova* expedition of 1910-1912 had as its main objective (in Scott's words) "to reach the South Pole, and to secure for the British Empire the honour of this achievement". He took dogs, ponies and primitive mechanised vehicles to assist in hauling the vast amount of equipment needed to construct huts and stage depots, and a team including scientists to carry out exploration work (which Scott insisted on maintaining even in the knowledge that the Norwegian Amundsen was also racing to reach the Pole).

Scott and four others finally reached the Pole in January 1912, only to find the Norwegian flag flying – Amundsen had reached it five weeks earlier. But though demoralised and facing worsening weather, they found time to dig up and add to their burden some tree fossils, which were found with their bodies and proved to be of great geological importance.

This monument stands in splendid isolation overlooking the lower Hamoaze and Mount Edgcumbe Park. It deserves to be better known.

86. MOUNT WISE REDOUBT

Former telegraph station now marked with a landmark sculpture

Mount Wise was named after the Lord of the Manor of Stoke Damerel, Sir Thomas Wise (c.1576-1630) of Sydenham, near Tavistock, who built a mansion on this ridge of ground looking across to Mount Edgcumbe. Contemporary paintings show it surrounded by open fields, with only a handful of cottages and barns where Devonport now stands. The land later passed by inheritance to the Morice family before being sold to Sir John St Aubyn, who made a fortune selling land around Plymouth Dock to the government for military use.

The fortification of the Dockyard from the mid-eighteenth century made Mount Wise an important strategic point for protection against attack from the sea. An octagonal redoubt with stone walls was built here in the 1770s, with eight 32-pounder guns and two 10-inch mortars. The guns would have commanded the Narrows so that any enemy ships venturing into the Tamar could be disabled while they were still negotiating the awkward eddies and strong tidal flows between Devil's Point and Wilderness Point.

The development of a semaphore signalling system by the Chappe brothers in Revolutionary France in the 1790s enabled the French government to communicate rapidly with administrative and military centres across the country. A chain of semaphore stations within sight of each other sent messages using moveable arms and a cross-bar, the signals being read with the aid of a codebook and standard symbols. A message from Paris could reach Lyons (a distance of over 300 miles by coach) in about 9 minutes.

The merits of this were not lost on the British Admiralty, and a similar system was set up to enable Whitehall to communicate with the country's main naval bases. News of Trafalgar and the death of Nelson in 1805 had taken 38 hours to reach London from Falmouth by coach. In 1806 a semaphore signalling station was built within Mount Wise Redoubt, the last of a series of 32 linking Plymouth Dock with London. In clear weather the system was invaluable, but fog, rain, or strong winds made the system useless, and contributed to errors and 'Chinese whispers'. London in particular was liable to fog from coal smoke or low cloud, and Admiralty records show that communication was only possible about 60% of the time.

The invention of the electric telegraph by Morse and Vail in 1837 rendered the semaphore system obsolete, and in 1852 the semaphore station at Mount Wise was replaced by a Morse telegraph which remained in use until the 1930s.

The former semaphore and telegraph station is commemorated by a 130ft-high mast erected in 1998, with a viewing platform giving fine views across to the Royal William Yard and out through the Narrows to the Sound. The base which supported the tall semaphore mast can still be seen inside the Redoubt, as well as stanchions for Second World War barrage balloons.

87. BOGEY KNIGHT'S STORE, MUTTON COVE

Fascinating 'Aladdin's Cave' selling military uniforms and equipment

The oldest military surplus store in Britain is hidden behind a narrow arch at Mutton Cove, formerly the entrance to Mount Wise Barracks. The firm of W & H Knight, Family Furniture Removers was established in 1898 by Harold and William Knight, trading from 52 Charlotte Street, Morice Town, but at some stage they branched out into government surplus supplies.

The business became known as 'Bogey Knight's' (probably the nickname of one of the Knight family) and moved to the present site in 1953. They have large stocks of genuine government surplus, including police, navy and general military clothing and equipment, together with new and used chandlery for ships and boats. Here you can find USAF jumpsuits and old police helmets, all-weather gear and billycans, ships' hawser and mooring buoys, red banded peaked caps, piles of shackles and drawers full of huge bolts, boots of all types and strangely-wrought things of mysterious purpose.

People come to Bogey Knight's for many things – some to look and some to buy. It is a favourite destination for set dressers in the film industry, as well as yacht owners looking for that elusive part they need.

There is a story that Arthur Knight (the son of Harold Knight) would tell his customers that Bogey Knight's was known and loved throughout the Royal Navy, and that naval vessels would always salute it as they passed. When a warship came by, he would rush his customers down to Mutton Cove, where he would stand on the quayside and solemnly take the salute. Sure enough, the ship's deck would be lined with sailors in the best uniforms, rigidly saluting, while the ship's pennants flew and the ensign was dipped. He knew, of course, that in fact they were saluting Admiralty House nearby, the home of Flag Officer Plymouth, but no doubt many of his customers were impressed.

Little remains of the former Mount Wise Barracks apart from the entrance arch and some of the perimeter wall. Originally the archway led into the Royal Laboratory, built for the Board of Ordnance in about 1804 during the long years of war with France. Despite its name, it was an armaments factory, making cartridges for cannon and muskets, and casting bullets and cannon balls for military use. The work was carried out in sheds which were separated from each other to minimise the risk of an explosion destroying the whole complex.

By 1834 the site had been enlarged and converted into barracks. The small yard occupied by Bogey Knight's became the stable-yard, the main entrance to the barracks being near to the Redoubt. The rest of the former barracks area was converted into residential housing in the 1970s and 80s.

The Knight family continued to run the business until 2020 when it was taken over by the Tunks.

88. FOULSTON'S KER STREET, DEVONPORT

Where some of John Foulston's finest public buildings survive

Here at Ker Street is what little remains of John Foulston's civic architecture that survived the Blitz and the post-war redevelopment of Plymouth. Ker Street was the administrative centre of the town of Devonport until the amalgamation of the Three Towns in 1914.

From its humble beginnings in the late 1600s as a mere 'garrison town', Plymouth Dock gradually grew in importance and civic pride, and that pride expressed itself in Foulston's designs for Ker Street. Dominating the site is the Guildhall, built in 1821 in Grecian style with four massive Doric pillars supporting the portico, surmounted by a statue of Britannia. Fortunately the building survived the Blitz undamaged, and has recently been restored.

In addition to a spacious main hall, the Guildhall included the Mayor's Parlour, where the town council met, rooms for the judges and magistrates who dealt with the Quarter Sessions and Police Court, offices for the overseers of the poor, and store rooms for lamps and road-mending tools. It also housed the police station and nine cells, and the 'parish engine' or pump used by the fire brigade. It is said that Devonport Guildhall was where the word dinosaur (meaning 'terrible lizard') was first used, in a talk on fossil finds given in 1841 by Sir Richard Owen, a famous naturalist.

Local pride in their fine new Guildhall prompted the town to petition King George IV to change its name from Plymouth Dock to Devonport, and this was granted in 1824. To celebrate this, a subscription was raised to build a monumental column on the nearby rock where a windmill had stood, and Foulston was asked to design it. This Doric column is over 100' high and includes an internal spiral staircase to a viewing gallery with excellent views across the Dockyard and out to the Sound. Access can be obtained from the Column Bakehouse in the ground floor of the Guildhall. It was intended that a statue of George IV would stand on top, but the money proved insufficient and the column remains empty. It was completed in 1827. In 1849 it was used for one of the world's first demonstrations of electric lighting.

Foulston also designed the neo-classical houses which used to line what was a very fashionable street. Sadly, many of these were damaged in the Blitz, and instead of being rebuilt they were demolished and replaced with monotonous four-storey blocks of flats. By the late twentieth century, Ker Street had become an area with significant social problems and anti-social behaviour, and recently these blocks have in turn been demolished and replaced with housing more appropriate in scale.

The only other Foulston-designed building which survives here is the Egyptian House, built in 1823 as a subscription school. It later became a library, and later still the Odd Fellows Hall. There is a similar building in Penzance which may also have been designed by Foulston. Unlike the Penzance version, the Devonport one is now looking rather neglected.

89. FORMER UNITARIAN CHAPEL, GEORGE STREET

Former Unitarian chapel, now a Co-op store

The Unitarian movement which started in sixteenth century Poland promoted the concept that God is one being, rejecting both the doctrine of the Trinity and the Christian belief in the deity of Christ. Unitarians held that although Jesus was a central figure in humanity's spiritual journey, he was wholly human. Unitarians also believed in universal salvation and the essential worthiness of human beings. The past tense is used, because although the Unitarian Church is still going strong, it no longer has any core beliefs: its members share their own individual beliefs and understanding of spiritual things. The Unitarian movement was considered heresy by the established church, and Unitarians were persecuted until the latter part of the eighteenth century.

The first Unitarian church in England was built in 1774, and one of its earliest adherents was Joseph Priestley, a scientist and philosopher who discovered oxygen and developed carbonated water. The movement became popular in Plymouth Dock, but construction of this chapel in George Street, Devonport in 1790 unfortunately coincided with a renewed period of persecution. Unitarianism attracted free-thinkers and radicals who were strong supporters of the libertarian principles of the French Revolution, and after the execution of Louis XVI in Paris in 1793 and the naval mutinies of the 1790s there was an increasing intolerance of dissent. Three members of the sect were executed as ringleaders in a 'most disgraceful riot' in Birmingham in 1791.

At some point in the late 1790s, soon after the chapel was built, the Commissioner of Plymouth Dock made it clear that any employee who attended the chapel would be sacked as a 'disloyal subject'. The congregation abandoned their chapel and continued to meet in secret, and ten years after it was built, the chapel was sold and was converted to a store for the sale of wines and spirits, thus changing its use from the spiritual to the spirituous. This would have been a sad day indeed for the Unitarians after all the work and money they must have put into its construction, since like most non-conformists they were staunch teetotallers. The old chapel remained a pub for over 100 years.

The Plymouth Mutual Co-operative & Industrial Society was started in 1860, but its first venture in Devonport ended in disaster. A Building Society forming part of the group was formed in 1866, and was contracted to build a sewer to the Stoke Military Hospital. Unhappily, although the quality of their workmanship was good they had badly underestimated the cost of the work and the Building Society became insolvent.

The first Co-op store in Devonport opened in 1877. More recently the old Unitarian chapel was acquired and is now a busy supermarket. The mutual and profit-sharing principles behind the Co-operative movement would no doubt have pleased the Unitarians who erected this fine building.

90. RAGLAN BARRACKS GATEHOUSE

The site of Devonport's largest barracks, designed by Francis Fowke

The improvements to the dockyard's defences under Colonel Dixon in 1779 also resulted in the building of no less than six barrack squares behind the Lines: Marlborough and Granby to the north, then Frederick, Ligonier and Cumberland to the east, and the George Barracks to the south. Perhaps predictably, the sudden influx of hundreds of soldiers led to increasing trouble in the town, and it was found necessary to erect a 12ft high wall behind the barracks area to segregate the army from the civilians.

Francis Fowke (1823-1865) was one of the pre-eminent architects of the mid nineteenth century, responsible for designing the Victoria & Albert Museum, the building for the 1862 International Exhibition (parts of which were incorporated into the Alexandra Palace), and his crowning achievement, the Royal Albert Hall.

Fowke was also a Captain in the Royal Engineers, and in 1853 he received his first major commission, to design a new barracks at Devonport. The Frederick, Ligonier and Cumberland barracks, which were by then little more than 'dilapidated huts', were pulled down and replaced with a substantial barracks named after Lord Raglan, the commander of the British forces in the Crimean War of 1853 to 1856. A fine Gatehouse in the Baroque style surmounted by a clock-tower led into an enormous parade-ground, the largest in Plymouth, surrounded by brick-built barracks. Some of them were in the 'Indian' style with flat roofs and verandahs, giving rise to a story that they had originally been intended for use in India, but by some mix-up ended up here instead. They provided accommodation for two regiments of the line, or 2,000 men and 80 officers.

The barracks were demolished in the 1960s for housing, and only the gatehouse remains, together with a section of the wall behind the Devonport Playhouse. The gatehouse has been described as "one of the most impressive barrack entrances and guardhouses in England".

Francis Fowke was a remarkably inventive architect who was a forerunner in the use of new materials and techniques, particularly in the use of gas lighting and ventilation systems. He introduced terracotta into building design, most obviously in the frieze around the Royal Albert Hall, and experimented with the architectural use of iron.

As well as his architectural achievements, Fowke is credited with the invention of the bellows camera, an improved portable fire-engine and a collapsible canvas pontoon to speed up the construction of temporary bridges for military use. He was described by a contemporary engineer as "a man of science, possessing a fertility of invention which amounted to genius". Sadly he died suddenly in 1865 at the age of only 42 before many of his projects could be completed.

91. OLD MIDLAND BANK, FORE STREET

The old commercial heart of Devonport, destroyed by bombs and the MOD

While the elegant administrative part of Devonport was at Ker Street, its main shopping centre and commercial heart was Fore Street, which ran from the Dockyard Gate (now South Yard) up to the drawbridge through the Lines and on to Paradise Road running east towards Plymouth.

Here, before the Second World War, were the large department stores – J B Love, Boold's, Tozers – and here or in adjacent streets were the theatres and cinemas: the Tivoli, the Alhambra, the Hippodrome, the Electric, the Forum. Here was the Post Office, Boots, Woolworths and Marks & Spencer, banks and public houses, drapers and tailors and butchers and cafes and hairdressers, and all the shops and offices which a large town needed. Here you could catch a tram to Derry's Cross, Peverell or North Road Station, or get your laundry cleaned.

The Blitz changed all that. Having devastated the centre of Plymouth, the Germans turned their attention to Devonport in April 1941. On one night, 23 April, wave after wave of bombers flew over the civilian areas for six hours of hellish destruction. The entirety of Fore Street west of Chapel Street was destroyed with hardly a wall left standing, apart from a forlorn group of buildings at the top end. One of those was the Midland Bank, with Woolworth's and Marks & Spencer on either side of it.

One Devonport resident wrote: "We had spent the night sleeping on Bere Alston railway station because Lord Haw-Haw had warned the citizens of Devonport that their town was going to be destroyed. We came back the next day and the heart of Devonport was gone. Everything was either burning, standing as a shell, or completely flattened. Our house and shop was a flat pile of bricks. All we had were the clothes we were wearing and the little money mum had in her purse. She sat on the edge of the pavement and cried".

The end of the war on VE Day saw the beginning of the reconstruction of Plymouth's centre, but there was no such hope for Devonport. The Admiralty requisitioned 50 acres of the civilian part of the town for Dockyard expansion, including Fore Street and its adjoining streets. The authors of the Plan for Plymouth shrugged their shoulders: "The elimination of the main shopping centre at Devonport, also destroyed but not to be rebuilt owing to the requirements of the Dockyard, will lead to the concentration of a greater area of shopping floor space in the new Plymouth centre". In 1957 the notorious Wall took shape, with its notices stating 'Keep Out – Admiralty Property', and Devonport died.

In 2004 the land was finally released for residential development, and the Wall came down in 2007. Fore Street has been rebuilt with pleasant terraced houses, and only the façade of the old Midland Bank remains, still with its 'Night Safe' to enable shopkeepers to deposit the day's takings after close of business, to remind us of Devonport's former glory.

92. NORTH CORNER AND CORNWALL BEACH

The first residential area at Plymouth Dock

North Corner is where the civilian town of Devonport started. The construction of the first dockyard just south of here in the 1690s necessitated the building of houses for the dockyard workers, who were initially living aboard floating hulks (old warships with masts, rigging and cannon removed). A dockyard needed ropemakers, blacksmiths, carpenters, sailmakers, braziers and armourers, as well as stevedores and general labourers. The place was called North Corner because it was in the corner formed by the northern dockyard wall and the banks of the Tamar.

When the New Gun Wharf or Morice Yard was later built just to the north, North Corner was forever sandwiched between the walls surrounding the two yards, and as the numbers employed in the Yard increased, so the town spread to the east, up Queen Street to Morice Square and Fore Street.

The quayside is known as Cornwall Beach because this was one of the points at which a ferry across the Tamar into Cornwall could be hired. Many of the watermen and women who plied their trade on the Hamoaze lived here and kept their boats on the beach below the quay. North Corner was where market garden produce from the Tamar Valley was unloaded and taken to Devonport market, and this helped to make it the main commercial wharf for the town. The volume of traffic to and from here led to the installation of a pontoon in 1883 which has recently been renewed, although now it is only used by fishermen.

The importance of North Corner and the crossing into Cornwall is demonstrated by the fine series of semi-circular steps leading down to the beach, built in cut granite some time in the nineteenth century. The Steam Packet Inn and the former Swan Hotel opposite to it probably date in part from the early 1700s, while the ornamental red-brick Piermaster's House was built in 1899. There was a strong community of fishermen, boatmen and local traders which survives today among those with long memories.

Sadly Cornwall Beach today is overshadowed by a truly monstrous concrete bridge built by the MOD in 1963, providing a road link between Morice Yard and South Yard. This dominates the historic part of North Corner, throwing a malign shadow across the beach and quay and destroying the outlook across the Hamoaze. Cornwall Beach is now a sad, blighted corner of Devonport, filled with rotting hulks and rubbish, with rusty boat-trailers parked under the grey concrete spans of the bridge.

This bridge is typical of the MOD's post-war disdain for Devonport's residents. The South Yard extension, that unforgiveable act of governmental vandalism, has recently been given back to the town; the infamous Wall has come down, and new housing built under the aegis of the Devonport Urban Regeneration scheme has provided homes for more than 1,100 people. But this monstrosity at North Corner remains, lest we forget.

93. MORICE YARD GATEHOUSE, QUEEN STREET

The best-preserved part of the old Dockyard, formerly the Gun Wharf

In the early 1700s it became necessary to extend the old Gun Wharf, which stood below Mount Wise where the Mayflower Marina apartment block now stands. The Board of Ordnance was unable to persuade the Edgcumbes, who owned the land, to sell or lease any additional space, so the decision was taken in 1718 to build a new Gun Wharf immediately upstream of North Corner. Even this land could only be had by leasing it from Sir Nicholas Morice. Surprisingly, until the nineteenth century much of the land at Devonport was held under leases from the Morice, St Aubyn or Edgcumbe families. Even today, much of Devonport remains in the hands of the St Aubyns.

The 'New Gun Wharf' (now known as Morice Yard) was, like the Dockyard, designed symmetrically, with a centrally placed Officers' Terrace looking down onto the Hamoaze. The officers' quarters were well-appointed, with their own 'Bogge Houses' at the back. At the wharf there were two small basins for loading ammunition barges, each with a four-storey warehouse adjoining. There was also a powder magazine, storage for gun barrels and other equipment, and a smithy for the armourer. The Yard was surrounded by a high stone wall with a gatehouse.

The Yard was described by Edward Hoxland in his 'Plymouth Dock Guide' of 1796: "[Here] a prodigious assortment of ammunition is constantly in store, as well as a great variety of arms of every description: cannons, cannonades [a short-barrelled cannon firing heavy shot, used for pounding ships at close-range], mortars [pot-shaped guns used for lobbing explosive shells into targets ashore], bombs, swords and almost every other device which has been contrived by man to take away the life of man". To avoid sparks which might ignite any gunpowder, all boots, swords or spurs had to be left at the gatehouse, where visitors were issued with wooden clogs.

The New Gun Wharf suffered major damage in 1799 when careless handling caused the fuses of some six-inch shells to be ignited. "The Three Towns were convulsed as by an earthquake as the fuses lit. The establishment was wrecked and the survivors witnessed a nightmare of flying limbs and maimed corpses – all so sudden and terrible that the number of victims has never been ascertained", wrote Hoxland.

Much of the original New Gun Wharf has survived, including the southern part of the old stone wall built of vertical pieces of shale, the Officers' Terrace and the two Georgian storehouses on the quayside. This is the original gatehouse, with cannons used as wheel guards to prevent damage to the stonework from cart-wheel bosses, an ornamental lamp bracket over the gates, and piers topped with mortars. Beyond the gates can be seen the yard bell and the wheel over which the bell-rope would have been wound, mounted on an iron pole. This bell would have been rung to signify the end of the working day, and also to summon help in the event of a fire.

94. FORMER ROYAL ALBERT HOSPITAL

Site of the Lock Ward where prostitutes were imprisoned

It was not until 1863 that Devonport got its own hospital, built by public subscription to provide an acceptable alternative to the infirmary at the Workhouse for the poor who were in need of treatment. It was named the Royal Albert Hospital after Prince Albert, whose death in 1861 had been followed by a tide of mourning and a plethora of memorials across the country, and the layout of the wards was planned by Florence Nightingale. The hospital was built between St Aubyn Road and the northern Lines, and parts of the surrounding wall remain, together with some of its Italianate towers.

As well as ordinary medical wards, the hospital was the first to be certified under the Contagious Diseases Act of 1864 for incarcerating women suspected of being prostitutes and having venereal disease, so that they could be treated. The incidence of syphilis in the armed forces (particularly those stationed at naval ports) had become a major concern to the authorities, and the Act enabled the police to arrest any woman suspected of being a prostitute and subject her to an intimate examination by a (male) police surgeon to determine if she had VD. If they considered that she did, then she would be sent to the 'Lock Ward'. This ward was subsidised by the government and provided the hospital with a much-needed source of revenue.

A formal enquiry into prostitution in 1862 had found that one-third of all servicemen needing hospitalisation suffered from VD, equivalent to the loss of two battalions every year. According to evidence submitted to the committee, there were some 900 prostitutes under the age of 15 in the Three Towns, and many of these plied their trade in the beer houses of Devonport, which were said to be little more than brothels. Prostitution in Britain was considered to have reached 'gigantic proportions', which "saps the vigour of our soldiers and seamen, sows the seeds of degradation and degeneracy, and causes an amount of suffering difficult to over-estimate". However the committee did not consider it would be fair to 'punish' servicemen by subjecting them to routine medical examinations.

For the dockyard police, the worst type of prostitute was what they called the 'tramp class' who "inhabit the lowest kind of brothel, hang about the fields at night, and get hold of men going home and intoxicated soldiers and sailors".

The Contagious Diseases Acts were resented by the civilian population as an infringement of civil liberty. Any woman on her own was liable to be arrested and subjected to a surgical examination, and those unfortunates who temporarily resorted to prostitution in difficult times to 'tide them over' found themselves stigmatised by incarceration in the Lock Wards, and forced into long term prostitution because they were unable to get any other employment. Following an increasingly vehement campaign the Acts were repealed in 1886.

The Royal Albert Hospital remained in use until 1981 when the new hub hospital at Derriford was opened.

95. TORPOINT FERRY

The biggest chain ferry operation in the world, and one of the earliest

By the 1820s the need arose for a bigger and more reliable ferry between Devonport and the new town of Torpoint. The nearest bridge across the Tamar from Devon into Cornwall was many miles upstream, at Gunnislake, and while there were ferry crossings at Saltash, Torpoint and Cremyll, these were small rowing boats dependent on wind and tide. The Torpoint ferry was by then carrying stage-coaches making use of the improvements to the turnpike west to Liskeard, and the owners of the ferry rights (the Earl of Mount Edgcumbe and Mr Pole Carew of Antony House) made enquiries about using a steam ferry like that which had recently been introduced across the River Tay in Scotland. A bridge was ruled out because the Admiralty required a full 100' clearance at high tide for the masts of warships.

James Meadows Rendel was a gifted civil engineer, who was born on an isolated farm near Drewsteignton in 1799. His father was a road surveyor as well as a farmer; James was educated at home by his mother, as the nearest school was too far away. He nevertheless managed to obtain a position as a trainee surveyor with the great Thomas Telford, and worked with him on roads and suspension bridges across Britain. His first completed project in Plymouth was his elegant cast iron road bridge of 1828 over the Plym at Laira, which was replaced by the present plain concrete bridge in 1961 and unceremoniously demolished. Only the stone-built approach on the Pomphlett side remains.

The first steam-powered chain ferry in the world was the Dartmouth Floating Bridge, now known as the Higher Ferry. It was opened in 1831 with Rendel as engineer. Two chains were laid across the river, anchored on each bank, and the twin-hulled floating bridge warped its way along the chains using a small steam engine and drive cogs mounted centrally, with narrow road-decks on either side. This was a method which had been proposed by the Scottish inventor of the steam hammer, James Nasmyth, for use on the Forth & Clyde Canal, but never built. Rendel realised that one of the chief advantages of a chain ferry was that the weight of the chains rising and falling to the river bed eliminated any obstruction to navigation, while the chains kept the ferry on course.

His next chain ferry was that at Saltash, using a similar design. This opened in 1833 but was soon closed for repair and ceased working four months later. It was not until 1850 that a new ferry service started, finally closing when the Tamar Road Bridge opened in 1961.

The steam-powered Torpoint Floating Bridge opened on 1 April 1834, capable of taking four carriages and horses, seven saddle-horses and 60 foot-passengers. Unlike that at Saltash, the Torpoint Ferry has continued to run from that day to this, and now has three modern ferries providing a crossing service round-the-clock. Each ferry carries up to 73 vehicles, with foot-passengers and cyclists travelling free.

96. KEYHAM VIADUCT, ST LEVAN ROAD

One of Brunel's timber fan viaducts converted to a girder bridge

The great engineer I K Brunel had the railway network in the South West well and truly in his pocket, not least because the further west the rails stretched, the more important it was to adopt his broad gauge system if the difficulties of a change of gauge were to be avoided. Thus having engineered both the Bristol & Exeter and the South Devon Railway from Exeter to Plymouth, he was appointed in 1845 by the Directors of the Cornwall Railway to construct a broad gauge line on from Plymouth, initially to the port of Falmouth.

Brunel's genius as an engineer was to combine a remarkable ability to achieve innovative solutions to engineering difficulties large and small, with an architect's eye for elegance and simplicity. He never built anything plain or ugly. Unfortunately the great advances in steel-making arrived just too late for any of his projects, and he had to improvise as best he could with timber, wrought and cast iron, and brick or stone.

With the line into Cornwall he faced an engineering conundrum. While the terrain was difficult to traverse, with numerous deep valleys running southwards from the high central spine requiring many viaducts and major earthworks, the county was relatively poor and the likely income from goods traffic could not justify high construction costs. Brunel's solution was to use 'fan timber' viaducts, with slender stone or timber piers rising to about 30' below rail level, supporting four braced timber struts splayed out like a fan, which in turn supported the timber deck on which the single rail track ran.

The viaduct at Keyham was one of the loftier ones, with the trains running some 90' above ground level. It would have been a sight to behold when a heavy broad gauge locomotive hauling a train of laden trucks or carriages ponderously traversed the viaduct, so high and so narrow, accompanied by a chorus of creaking and groaning timbers. Yet despite their slim elegance these timber fan viaducts supported ever-increasing weights and speeds without complaint or mishap until the need to convert the line from single to double track (and the growing cost of renewals) led to their replacement.

The fan timbers of the Keyham Viaduct were replaced with steel girders in 1900, and the photograph opposite shows how it was achieved with the minimum of interruption to trains. The existing piers were wide enough to support two standard gauge tracks, as standard gauge was only 2/3rds the width of broad gauge. They were built up with brick to just below rail level, leaving slots for the fan timbers, which continued to support the deck while steel X-frame girders were placed either side of it. Then the timber-work was removed and new decking installed, supported by these girders. The patches in the brickwork where the slots for the timber struts were later filled in can still be seen (as in the photograph opposite), above the original stone piers which continue to support the weight of trains some 160 years after they were built.

PLYMOUTH'S VICTORIAN TERRACED HOUSES

211

Northern Plymouth

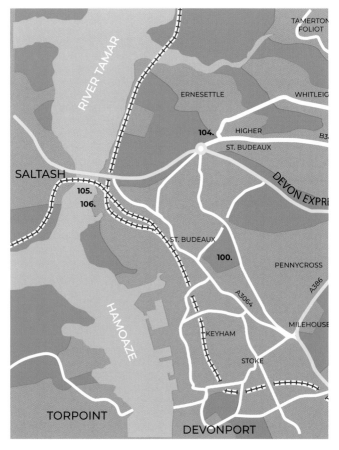

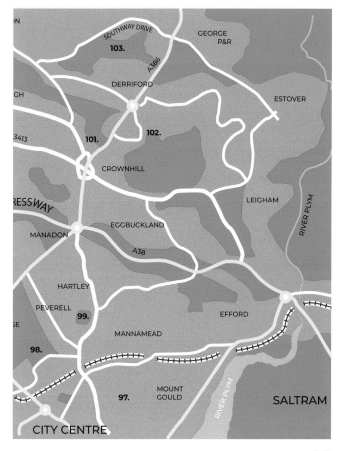

97. FREEDOM FIELDS PARK

Civil War battlefield, and Michael Foot's memorial

King Charles I was not popular in the town of Plymouth. His various naval expeditions from Plymouth against France and Spain were woefully underfunded, and what money there was had been embezzled by the naval administrator. In 1625 10,000 soldiers and 90 ships had been assembled to fight the Spanish, but the soldiers were left starving and without lodgings, stealing just to stay alive, or relying on the charity of the locals. Needless to say, the expedition was a complete disaster, as were subsequent ones, and Plymouth was forced to cope with thousands of sick and wounded men.

It is hardly surprising that in the Civil War of 1642 to 1646 Plymouth immediately declared for Parliament, and a vow was made to resist the King even if the town was razed to the ground. There were many battles in and around Plymouth, but the most famous was the Sabbath Day Battle in Freedom Fields in December 1643, when a surprise attack by the Royalists was defeated by a determined defence of Lipson Hill, and the siege of Plymouth was finally repulsed. It is usually assumed that this battle gave Freedom Fields its name, but in fact the name derives from the annual celebrations following the final defeat of the Breton raiders in 1403.

The park still has an essentially Victorian character, with its swan-neck lampposts, cast-iron seats and an ornamental shelter, surrounded by nineteenth century terraces.

The Labour politician Michael Foot was born in nearby Lipson Terrace in 1913, one of the seven children of Isaac Foot. Isaac was a colourful character, a bibliophile and lawyer who was the Liberal MP for Bodmin in the inter-war years and Lord Mayor of Plymouth in 1945. Michael Foot was a passionate orator whose strongly left-wing views placed him rather outside the mainstream. He started life as a journalist, opposing rearmament in the 1930s and arguing for unilateral disarmament. As a leader writer at the London Evening Standard in the war years, he coined the slogan 'Dig for Victory'.

He sat as Labour MP for Devonport from 1945 to 1955, and later as MP for Ebbw Vale in South Wales, serving in government under both Harold Wilson and James Callaghan. In 1980 he became the Leader of the Labour Party, and was responsible for the strongly socialist 1983 Labour manifesto (memorably described as 'the longest suicide note in history'), which advocated unilateral nuclear disarmament, abolition of the House of Lords, nationalisation of the banks and immediately withdrawal from what was then the European Economic Community. He resigned after the election when Labour achieved its lowest share of the vote since 1918.

Michael Foot was a lifelong atheist and republican, who remained true to his beliefs even though rather out of tune with the public mood. Indeed, his time as the party leader was not dissimilar to that of a more recent incumbent.

98. VICTORIAN CHAPEL, FORD PARK CEMETERY

Restored mortuary chapel with memorial naming civilian Blitz victims

Ford Park Cemetery, the oldest in Plymouth, is self-funding and separately run from the council-owned cemeteries at Efford and Weston Mill. It was opened in 1848 as the Plymouth, Stonehouse & Devonport Cemetery to alleviate overcrowding in the churchyards of the local parish churches which had become a national scandal. Its opening was timely, as it came into use during one of the worst outbreaks of cholera in the country, and during its first year received over 400 burials.

The cemetery was originally 18 acres but a further 16½ acres were added in 1875. In Victorian times it was the main cemetery for the Three Towns, and it is estimated that about a quarter of a million people are buried within its grounds. Separate areas were provided for Anglicans and Nonconformists, with two matching mortuary chapels. The Anglican one survives and was restored from semi-dereliction in 2010, but the Nonconformist one was destroyed by a jettisoned bomb in the Second World War and has been rebuilt in 1960s style.

During the 1970s and 80s the cemetery became overgrown and neglected because of poor management and a loss of revenue attributed to the popularity of cremation, and the cemetery company went into liquidation. A trust was set up to take over the ownership and management in 2000, supported by the Friends of Ford Park Cemetery. Under the Trust the cemetery has been reopened for burials, and with the assistance of grants and donations the site has been cleared of undergrowth and made safe.

There are walking trails around the Grade II* listed park taking in some of the graves of notable people, who include two holders of the Victoria Cross for Valour, Captain Andrew Henry, Royal Artillery, and Quartermaster George Hinckley, Royal Navy. Other notable graves include those of the Rev Stephen Hawker, Vicar of Morwenstowe and author of the Cornish anthem 'Song of the Western Men' ("And shall Trelawney die?"); Jimmy Peters, who in 1906 became the first black rugby player to play for England; the Plymouth department store proprietors John Yeo, Edward Dingle and J J Spooner; the Whiteleggs of circus fame; Dr Budd, the eccentric GP of Durnford Street with whom Conan Doyle worked for a time; Ann Farley, the original purveyor of Farley's Rusks; and Mabel Ramsey, a pioneering female surgeon who became the first surgeon-gynaecologist at Plymouth City Hospital.

There are Commonwealth War Graves Commission plots containing 771 graves from the First World War, 198 from the Second, and 1,098 non-war service burials. There are three French and two Russian graves among them.

The restored Victorian Chapel contains a memorial listing the names of all the 1,172 civilian victims of the Plymouth Blitz. It is used for religious or secular funeral or memorial services as well as concerts and other events. The other building contains an exhibition space as well as the trust's offices.

99. VICTORIAN URINAL, THORN PARK

One-man cylindrical cast iron urinal still in situ

This unusual single-user cast iron urinal stands in a secluded spot behind some evergreen shrubs in Thorn Park, Mannamead. It is one of only a handful of Victorian public urinals still standing in their original place, and believe it or not, it is a listed monument (Grade II).

It is a surprising object to find lurking in the bushes in a small residential park, and leaves one wondering why on earth it was put there? Were gentlemen in the habit of peeing in the shrubbery, alarming the matrons and the nannies pushing prams around the park by suddenly emerging from behind the bushes doing up their flies? Were there unpleasant smells and noises emanating from within the laurels? And why only in Thorn Park? Sadly, history does not record the reason for its existence.

It was manufactured at the Saracen Iron Foundry of Walter MacFarlane & Co of Glasgow in about 1910, and is in its original condition. A small cast iron lion's head allows rainwater to spout away from the foundations. Walter Macfarlane & Co were renowned for producing cast ironwork for architectural purposes, including lamp standards, railings, bandstands, verandas, drinking fountains and prefabricated buildings as well as urinals.

The flushing lavatory was invented by the great Victorian sanitary engineer, George Jennings, who exhibited the first public toilets at the Great Exhibition of 1851 in Hyde Park. His strangely-named 'monkey closets' were installed in the Retiring Rooms of the Crystal Palace. These were the first public toilets, and they caused great excitement. No less than 827,280 visitors paid one penny to use them, for which expenditure they got a clean seat, a towel, a comb and a shoe shine. The expression 'to spend a penny' became a euphemism for going to the lavatory.

The better-known and aptly-named Thomas Crapper later improved the flushing toilet and started a successful business manufacturing sanitary ware in 1861. He took out patents for the U-bend and the floating ballcock, and also invented the manhole cover. These developments coincided with a growing interest in public health and sanitation in line with the Victorian attitude to civilisation and propriety. The delicate patterns on the cast iron panels of this simple urinal reflect that civilising influence, just as they conceal the distasteful sight of bodily functions being exercised in public.

The disapproval of men urinating in public is not just a Victorian trait. In ancient Rome the Emperor Vespasian found the practice distasteful, and ordered the construction of public urinals flushed by running water for which the user had to pay a tax or fee. Even today in Italy public urinals are sometimes called 'Vespasiani'.

100. AGNES WESTON MEMORIAL, WESTON MILL

Memorial celebrating the founder of 'Aggies', the Royal Sailors' Rest

Agnes Weston was a big–hearted woman who devoted her life to philanthropic causes, especially temperance and the welfare of seamen. She understood that life at sea could be lonely and that many longed for news from home, while for their wives and families, life ashore could be bleak and impoverished.

Agnes was born in 1840 to a wealthy family. On leaving school she became involved in the temperance movement as a speaker and writer of tracts, and later opened a coffee shop in Bath (where her family then lived) for local soldiers. She began writing to her customers when they were posted abroad, and one of her letters was shown to a troopship steward who regretted that he had no one who wrote him letters like that. Agnes was told about the steward and she began writing to him and others.

In 1873 she came to Devonport to meet some of the sailors with whom she had corresponded. There she struck up a friendship with Sophia Wintz, who was also involved in the temperance movement. Agnes joined the Royal Naval Temperance Society which enabled her to visit warships in port and talk to the crews about the evils of drink. She and Sophia decided to open a sailor's hostel, and with the help of other members of the temperance movement they raised enough funds to buy a house in Fore Street, which opened in May 1876 as the 'Sailor's Rest', offering 'Coffee, Comfort and Company for One Penny' — a place to eat and drink (strictly non-alcoholic) and a bed for the night. Religious services were held in a hall at the back. The hostel proved so popular that an adjoining property was bought and the premises expanded.

In 1881 they opened a Sailor's Rest in Portsmouth, providing baths, lodgings and recreational activities. The success of the enterprise enabled them to acquire a much expanded site in Devonport at the bottom of Fore Street immediately outside the Dockyard Gate, where an impressive five-storey building was opened in the late 1880s with accommodation for 900 men. In 1892 by royal warrant the building was named 'Agnes Weston's Royal Sailor's Rest', although locally it was known affectionately as 'Aggie's'.

'Mother Weston' remained determined to advance the cause of temperance. A monthly journal *Ashore and Afloat* was distributed to encourage temperance, Christian beliefs and behaviour amongst sailors. She was a passionate advocate of the welfare of sailors and their families, and was instrumental in changing the system whereby sailors would only be paid off when the ship returned to port, to enable their families to be provided for while they were at sea.

Agnes Weston died at Devonport in 1918 and was buried in Weston Mill Cemetery with full naval honours. The Sailor's Rests continued to operate until the turn of the twenty-first century, when improved naval welfare provision made them redundant.

101. CROWNHILL FORT

The finest and the best-preserved of the Palmerston forts around Plymouth

The prospect of invasion by France had been a constant concern for the English right up to the end of the nineteenth century and the 'entente cordiale' of 1904. In 1852 Napoleon's nephew Louis Napoleon was proclaimed Emperor Napoleon III and the Second Empire was born. He made no secret of his imperial ambitions, and worked to reassert French influence in Europe and around the world. In 1858 France launched the first screw-driven armoured warship, *La Gloire,* which could outgun anything possessed by the Royal Navy. This appears to have galvanised the Prime Minister, Lord Palmerston, into setting up a Royal Commission to assess the country's coastal defences.

The Commission reported in 1860 that the existing defences of Plymouth and Portsmouth were inadequate to counter the modern warships which French had pioneered. Their recommendations included improving the security of Plymouth Sound as a safe anchorage (in particular the entrance to the Hamoaze), and protecting the Dockyard against a land attack following a landing in force at Whitsand Bay or elsewhere along the coast. They proposed a chain of 20 forts and batteries around Plymouth from Whitsand Bay to Staddon Point, as well as ten batteries around the Sound. Despite estimating the cost of the work in the colossal sum of £2,670,000, the work was put in hand without delay.

As we saw with the Royal William Yard, public works in the latter half of the nineteenth century were not done on the cheap. The forts and batteries had massive granite-faced ramparts backed by prodigious earthworks with elegant stone-built arched gatehouses, and still stand ready to repel invaders 150 years later. The huge fort at Tregantle (which remains in MOD hands) has a great bow-fronted keep or inner battery, so that even if the outer walls were breached the enemy would face withering cannon fire inside. Protected roads linked the batteries with the main forts. The familiar forts and batteries protecting the Sound, such as Picklecombe, Drake's Island, Bovisand and the Breakwater Fort, seem so solidly built that they will surely stand until the Last Trump.

To the north of Plymouth, between the Tamar and the Plym, was a chain of six forts and five batteries – Ernesettle, Agaton, Knowles, Woodland, Crownhill, Bowden, Eggbuckland, Forder, Austin, Efford and Laira. The largest and strongest of these was Crownhill Fort, which remains in its original condition as it was the Headquarters of the Plymouth Garrison until 1985, and was subsequently taken over by the Landmark Trust and restored. It has well-preserved Haxo casemates, and working replicas of the rifled muzzle-loading guns of the 1860s, together with a Moncrieff Counterweighted Disappearing Gun, which has a counterweight system enabling it to rise above the parapet to fire, with the recoil bringing the muzzle down below the parapet for reloading. The entrance arch is Norman in style.

The fort now provides self-catering accommodation and office and workshop space for small businesses.

102. THE SHIP, DERRIFORD

Plymouth's most remarkable new building, hidden from sight

In June 1991 workmen and excavators moved onto a field at the extremity of Brest Road in the Derriford Business Park, to build what would become one of the two most striking examples of modern architecture in Plymouth (the other being the University's Roland Levinsky Building at Drake Circus).

The building was the headquarters of the *Evening Herald* and the *Western Morning News,* both owned by Northcliffe Newspapers. It was designed by Sir Nicholas Grimshaw, a highly-regarded architect responsible for countless buildings around the world including the Eden Centre and Waterloo International. It won no less than four major architectural awards, including both the RIBA and the Royal Fine Art Building of the Year awards.

The exterior, encased in around 700 sheets of half-inch thick glass, resembles a glass aircraft carrier complete with island (control tower). The glass cladding is supported by 39 curved steel 'tusks'. Inside, it had 50 miles of cables linking around 400 computer workstations. It opened in 1993, and the total cost of construction was more than £33.5 million. It soon became known as 'The Ship'.

For such a landmark building, the site chosen was an odd one. There are few places in Plymouth where it would be less visible than here, on the far side of a business park and looking down into the unspoiled Bircham Valley. It cannot be seen from any of the approaches to Plymouth, and even local people would be forgiven for not knowing of its existence. The back of the building facing Brest Road looks like an ordinary steel-clad industrial warehouse.

Sadly, it proved to be something of a white elephant. The building was vacated in 2013 after only 20 years' use, following a change of ownership which resulted in newspaper staff being relocated to smaller offices at Millbay, and printing being carried out at a central plant rather than regionally. It was unsuccessfully advertised for sale, and in April 2015 the owners served Plymouth City Council with a notice of intention to demolish it. There was a public campaign to save it, stating that "The Western Morning News Building is Plymouth's most significant building of the late 20th century, and whilst it has not yet been formally recognised as a historic asset, this is surely only a matter of time. To permit its demolition would be to directly contradict the strategic ambition to enhance the role of historic assets, it would destroy the only existing landmark building in the area, and would not add richness to the local urban form".

Three months later, in July 2015, it was announced that the building had been listed Grade II* by Historic England, making it the UK's 'youngest' building to be listed, and preventing its destruction. It was bought by Burrington Estates, who initially had difficulty finding tenants, apart from a trampoline facility and a Clip-and Climb adventure centre. Fortunately in 2017 a call centre company, Sitel UK, opened a major branch there, and The Ship has once more become a thriving commercial hub.

103. PLYMOUTH MINIATURE STEAM, SOUTHWAY

A miniature steam railway in a parkland setting

What is it with the steam engine? Why are people so fascinated with it? Because it's the only machine made by human hands which seems alive – a living, breathing, fire-eating dragon. At rest, it simmers and hisses, and when the strain begins to tell, it huffs and puffs and pants like we do, exhaling clouds of steam from its iron lungs.

Plymouth's miniature steam enthusiasts have been running steam-powered trains since about 1970 when a raised track was built in Central Park, but construction of the Mayflower Sports Centre in 1981 meant that the group had to look for a new site. The place they eventually found did not look promising at first – it was on the edge of the city at Southway, and had been used as a council tip and somewhere to dump rubble from the blitzed city centre.

With the assistance of volunteers from the Manpower Services Commission's Youth Training Scheme, more than 3,500 tons of topsoil were brought in and landscaped to create an area of woodland and grass, and over half a mile of concrete track-bed was laid. The railway was opened in 1990. The area used by the railway is named Goodwin Park after the group's chairman, Sandy Goodwin, and now has mature trees and dense undergrowth to encourage wildlife.

The group's members include 'model engineers, steam enthusiasts and railway nuts'. Many of the locomotives and rolling stock have been built from scratch by members, and there are working steam traction engine models as well. Some work and training is carried out in workshops at the nearby Tor Bridge High School where an apprenticeship scheme is being run to introduce youngsters and adult members into engineering and practical skills. Plymouth Miniature Steam provides a source of enjoyment for those who like to work with their hands, and somewhere to walk for those who appreciate the woodland and grassland on their doorstep.

The railway is open to the public from April to October on the first and third Sundays in each month. A round trip is surprisingly extensive, taking you on a six minute journey in the form of a double loop through woodland and grassland, over bridges and through a short tunnel back to the station. There are colour-light signals, and part of the track is laid for no less than three gauges, 3½", 5" and 7¼", with mixed-gauge pointwork of amazing complexity. There is parking and a tea room at the station.

Southway Valley is a valuable recreational area, and is a designated nature reserve, home to woodland flowers like the common spotted orchid, bluebell, primrose, yellow pimpernel, wild garlic and pignut. There is also a new community orchard with old West Country varieties of fruit tree, planted and cared for by local residents and groups.

104. ST BUDEAUX CHURCH

Where Drake was married, and site of a key Civil War battle

The settlement of St Budeaux was founded in 480 AD, when the Breton bishop St Budoc sent some monks to Britain to found a Christian community. They landed at Ernesettle Creek and built a small church, probably of wattle, which was replaced with a stone one some time before the Norman invasion.

In Tudor times it was decided to build a new church on the higher ground away from the river, and the present building was erected in 1563. This building would have been new when Francis Drake married Mary Newman here in 1569. It appears that her family came from St Budeaux. She was buried here in 1583 although her grave is no longer evident.

St Budeaux appears to have been adopted as the spelling of the place as a more elegant form of St Budoc's, but the local pronunciation varies between St Boodow and St Buddox. The latter is closer to the original.

This church was a battleground during the Civil War of 1642 to 1651. While Plymouth was strongly supportive of the Parliamentarian cause, Cornwall was a Royalist stronghold, and the church was of considerable strategic importance, standing as it does on a prominent bluff overlooking the River Tamar above Saltash. In early 1644 a party of Royalists crossed the river and managed to secure the church and garrison it, enabling them to command the Tamar estuary so that a strong attack could be mounted against Plymouth from the north.

On 16 April 1644 Lieutenant Colonel Martin, the commander of the Parliamentary forces at Plymouth, sent 600 musketeers with 120 horsemen to attack the Royalists holding St Budeaux church. Because of a mistake made by their guides, the mounted soldiers appear to have lost their way and the foot soldiers got there first. Despite this setback, the foot soldiers were able to take the Cavalier garrison by surprise and recapture the church, taking 46 prisoners, three barrels of gunpowder, 20 horses and a quantity of weapons.

But that was not the end of the matter. On 27 December 1644 the Royalists crossed the Tamar from Cornwall in strength and marched towards the church, which had been heavily fortified by the Parliamentary contingent stationed there, with a defensive wall running west from the church tower. After a fierce battle lasting an hour and a half, the Royalists managed to retake the church. During the battle the church was badly damaged, and it was rebuilt in 1655.

To the north of the church the fields still slope down towards the Tamar, much as they did in the 1640s. There is an earth bank alongside the graveyard to the west which may date originally from the Civil War, although it also provided cover for the military road built in the 1860s to link the northern Palmerston fortifications from Ernesettle Battery to Laira.

105. ROYAL ALBERT BRIDGE

IK Brunel's last work, and a remarkable survival of early railway engineering

History has been kinder to Brunel's legacy than to that of his contemporaries. So many of his greatest works survive, sometimes (as with the SS *Great Britain*) against all the odds. The Royal Albert Bridge is one of these, still carrying trains into Cornwall with little visual modification more than 160 years after it was built.

For the crossing of the Tamar the Admiralty required a clear headroom of 100 feet above high water and a navigable width of 400 feet so that sailing vessels with their lofty masts could be brought upriver. This meant that a high-level bridge with long spans was needed, and the only suitable place where the river is narrow enough and the sides sufficiently steep to avoid the need for lengthy approach works is at Saltash. Here the river is some 370 yards wide and 70 feet deep at high water.

Such a crossing was not unprecedented. In 1850 the Britannia Bridge carrying the Chester & Holyhead Railway over the Menai Straits into Anglesey had been completed by that other great railway pioneer, Robert Stephenson. Stephenson was faced with a similar difficulty, namely the requirement that the Straits remain navigable to shipping. The topography was similar, but Stephenson had two great advantages over Brunel – first, there was a conveniently-sited shoal at mid point on which a central pier could be constructed, and second, the Chester & Holyhead Railway had the Irish Mail contract and so was considerably better funded than the impoverished Cornwall Railway.

Brunel was familiar with Stephenson's work and indeed had been present when the Britannia's massive box girders were floated into position, but the spans he designed were very different to those at Menai. Using a hollow tube to contain the force of compression along the top of each truss and suspension chains to contain the tensile force along the bottom, he managed to reduce the weight of each span to about two-thirds of that at Menai, thereby achieving a considerable saving of construction costs.

The more challenging task was building the central pier, which is about 180 feet from bedrock to rail level (about the height of the Guildhall tower). Over two-fifths is underwater and subject to strong tidal movement for much of the day. Brunel used an iron caisson with compressed air which was lowered into the mud to enable workmen to excavate the stinking ooze until the lower rim rested on the bedrock beneath. Then the granite pier was built up within the caisson until it was several feet above high water, to form the base for the four linked octagonal cast iron columns supporting the trusses, each 100 feet high and weighing about 100 tons.

The Royal Albert Bridge was the last of the great wrought-iron bridges of the Railway Age. It was opened by Prince Albert in May 1859, but Brunel was too ill to attend. He had himself carried over the bridge on a couch fitted to a flat truck, so he could take a last look at his completed masterpiece before his death later that year.

106. SALTASH PASSAGE D-DAY HARD

Where American GIs left for the Normandy beaches in 1944

Vicarage Road / US Army Route No.23 / Normandy Hill – the steep lane running down to Saltash Passage at St Budeaux has been called all these. On 6 June 1944 general infantrymen from the 4th Division of the US V and VII Corps marched down here to embark on landing craft and be ferried across the Channel to Normandy, taking with them all the equipment they needed, and handcarts loaded with ammunition boxes.

D-Day was the start of the final phase of the Second World War in Europe. In a little over three weeks Operation Overlord landed more than 850,000 men on the beachheads of Normandy, together with about 150,000 tanks and heavy vehicles and 570,000 tons of supplies. Plymouth was the embarkation point for 36,000 of these soldiers. The scale of the operation is difficult to imagine. Someone who was a child at the time remembers watching a seemingly endless convoy of American army lorries and military vehicles rumbling into Plymouth along Tavistock Road, line after line of them, hour after hour, carrying thousands of GIs with their heavy packs and rifles.

In November 1943 the US Navy set up an advanced amphibious base at Queen Anne's Battery with some 2,375 personnel. Their primary role was to organise the construction of the numerous hards (slipways) around Plymouth and elsewhere along the coast of Devon and Cornwall, so that hundreds of landing craft could embark soldiers and equipment for the assault on German-occupied France. Part of the Allied forces were to be landed on D-Day to secure the necessary beachheads, with the remainder of the soldiers, tanks and weapons brought ashore over the following weeks.

These hards were constructed using bulldozers, with a concrete apron above the high water mark and 'hardening mats' – reinforced concrete blocks hooked together – to cover the tidal foreshore. At Saltash Passage the hardening mats are still in use, looking like blocks of yellow chocolate.

Camps were built in Devon and Cornwall to accommodate the GIs. Where the toll barriers and offices for the Tamar Bridge now stand, there was an army base known as US Army Vicarage Road Camp. There was also a base for servicing and repair of landing craft on the Cornish side, just upstream of the Tamar Bridge.

Training for the American GIs to prepare them for what they would encounter in Normandy was undertaken on Bodmin Moor and Dartmoor, and also at Slapton Sands, which bore a slight resemblance to the Normandy beaches. Some villages and hamlets were cleared of occupants so that training with live ammunition could be carried out. There were inevitably casualties.

Nearby is the Ferry Inn and the slipway for the Saltash chain ferry. You can still see one of the hawse-holes with grooves cut by the ferry chain as it emerged from the anchor-point buried beneath the roadway.

Eastern Plymouth, Plympton & Plymstock

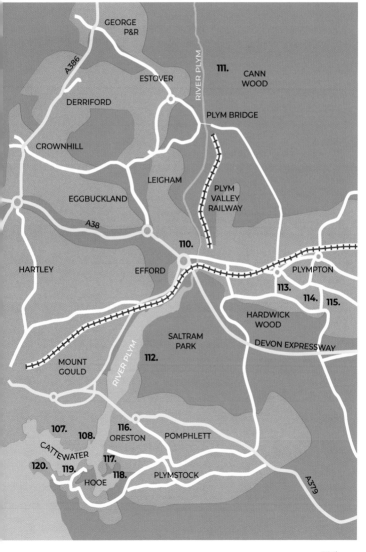

107. BREAKWATER HILL, CATTEDOWN

Where stone for the Breakwater was quarried, now part of the S W Coast Path

This strange stub of a road (now closed to vehicles) is part of the South West Coast Path, England's longest waymarked footpath, which stretches for 630 miles from Minehead in Somerset westwards to Land's End, and then eastwards along the south coast of Cornwall and Devon to Poole Harbour in Dorset, taking in some of the finest coastal scenery in the country. It has many ups and downs, and walking from one end to the other is said to be like climbing up and tramping down Mount Everest four times. It regularly features in lists of the world's best walks.

The South West Coast Path reaches Plymouth at Admiral's Hard, Stonehouse (the Cremyll ferry is officially part of the route) and continues around Mill Bay, the Hoe and Sutton Harbour to Cattedown and Pomphlett, leaving the boundary of the city at a 'welcome mat' at Jennycliff. Along the way there are plaques and sculptures of all sorts. Here at Breakwater Hill there is a Green Man lamp-post, two coastal beacons looking like rockets, and this medallion of St Christopher, patron saint of travellers.

There are fine views from here over the Barbican and the Cattewater, and it is a popular place from which to see the British Fireworks Championships, held at Mount Batten every August. What is not so evident is that for much of the way the narrow lane is edged with vertical drops on each side.

Once upon a time, grassy hills much like the Hoe bounded the Cattewater on each side, and this lane wandered over the pastures of Cattedown with only sheep and the odd shepherd for company. But beneath the turf lay easily-accessible sources of the grey Plymouth limestone. As industrialisation gathered pace in the nineteenth century, the need for large quantities of rock for building purposes and in particular for constructing the Breakwater between 1812 and 1841 led to extensive quarrying. By the time the quarries were exhausted, all that was left was this lane, perched high up above the quarry floors as if on a plinth. The quarry floors are now covered with warehouses and oil storage tanks.

About two million tons of rock were needed to build the Breakwater. It was dropped from barges into deep water to form an artificial reef. The elder John Rennie, the engineer responsible for it, devised a system to speed up the process, using a horse tramway at the quarries to carry the large blocks to the quayside, where the trucks were hauled onto specially-designed transport barges without needing cranes. The vessels would be moored stern-on to the quay and the loaded trucks would be brought in through stern ports and run down into the hold, which could contain eight loaded trucks either side of the stepped masts. The barges would then sail to the Breakwater site and the blocks would be tipped into the sea from each truck using a hinged platform. In this way 80 tons of stone could be discharged every 45 minutes, and the barges were able to make four trips a day.

108. CATTEDOWN BONE CAVES

A Stone Age cave system, now a national monument

In 1886 quarrymen working near Cattedown Road broke through into a fissure in the rock, revealing a limestone cave system. A well-known local archaeologist, R N Worth, examined the caves and discovered a wealth of fossils, including woolly rhinoceroses and mammoths from the Ice Age, cave lions, hyenas, wolves and bison, together with human bones. He and his colleagues exhumed the fossilised skeletons of at least 15 hominins (human-like primates) ranging from children to the elderly.

The caves are part of an extensive system of caverns and fissures thought to spread beneath the Cattedown area down to around 160 feet below sea level. In the Ice Age the sea level was about 200 feet lower than today, and the Plym at Cattewater ran through a deep gorge between high limestone cliffs. Part of the cave system is the Cattedown Reindeer Rift, where reindeer bones carbon-dated at 14,500 years old were found in the 1970s.

Today the caves – listed as a national monument by Historic England – remain fenced off, with the precise location kept secret to avoid the area being ransacked by fossil-hunters, and only a select few have been allowed inside them since their discovery. Further fossil remains were discovered recently after an investigation by members of Devon Karst Research Society.

Experts at Plymouth University and Oxford Brookes University have worked together to try to date some of the bone fragments, but dating is complicated by the fact that many fossils were broken and scorched during the Blitz when the Plymouth Athenaeum, where they were being stored, was bombed. A range of methods including non-contact 3D laser scanning has been used to reconstruct the missing parts of bones. The fact that human remains were found among Ice Age animal fossils suggests that 'Cattedown Man' was more than 10,000 years old. Woolly rhinos and cave lions are thought to have existed in Britain until around 35,000 years ago.

The caves discovered by the quarrymen in 1887 were big enough for people to live inside. Small pieces of charcoal were found in them, indicating that the early humans were making fires, so presumably they were cave-dwellers. Plymouth would have been very cold back then, and caves would have provided warmth and shelter. They would also have provided homes for cave lions and woolly rhinos, and later for packs of hyenas. It is not known how they perished – possibly they drowned when heavy rainfall caused floodwater to rise rapidly, or perhaps there was a rockfall which trapped them. Their remains cannot have been disturbed for tens of thousands of years, as the caves only came to light when the surrounding rock had been excavated.

The material from the caves is the largest collection of early human remains found in the UK, and when analysis is complete, they should be able to tell us a great deal about some of Western Europe's earliest people.

109. LEIGHAM TRAMWAY TUNNEL

One of the earliest railway tunnels, with a strange wartime secret

This is the north-east portal of Leigham Tunnel, one of the oldest railway tunnels in existence and among the longest tunnels to have been built in the earliest days of railways, when horses were more common as a means of motive power than steam locomotives.

The world's first railway tunnel was the Fritchley Tunnel in Derbyshire, built in 1793 for the Butterley Gangroad, but that is a mere 25 yards long. The first substantial tunnel was Hay Hill Tunnel of 1810 on the Pullo Pill Railway in the Forest of Dean, which was an astonishing 1,083 yards long. Next was the 674 yard tunnel at Talyllyn opened in 1816 as part of the Brecon to Hay tramway. Leigham Tunnel is 620 yards long, and was completed in 1823 by the Plymouth & Dartmoor Railway as part of its route from Sutton Harbour to Princetown.

The original survey for the line between Crabtree (Marsh Mills) and Jump (now Roborough) took the line up the Forder Valley to Fursdon and the George Hotel, but route was too steep for horse traction. Accordingly the route had to be changed to reduce the gradient, although this required a tunnel under Higher Leigham Farm and added substantially to the cost of the line. Construction started in 1822 with the sinking of a shaft half-way along the route, so that tunnelling could progress in both directions.

The north-east portal of the tunnel is beside the lane from Plym Bridge to Leigham. The south-west portal is just below Sheepstor Road where it leaves the B3432.

Leading a team of horses hauling heavy wagons through a tunnel of this length must have been challenging, but fortunately the tunnel is straight and a pinprick of light would always have been visible ahead.

The tunnel was abandoned when the tramway closed in 1883, although the rails were not lifted until 1916. That would have been the end of it, except that the savagery of the Blitz in the Second World War led the War Department to consider the need for a deep shelter for dockyard workers at Devonport if the bombing worsened. Why they chose a damp railway tunnel such a long way from Devonport is not known, but it was fitted with blast doors, emergency exits, bunks and accommodation for up to 3,000 people. Those who have explored inside the tunnel report that some of the adaptations remain, including hospital sick bays complete with curtain rails, and bed frames scattered around. Ladders still lead up to emergency exit points.

From 1944 when the air raids ceased it was used by the navy as storage for depth charges. In the 1950s it was noted in the government's Central Register of Underground Accommodation as a possible deep shelter in the event of a nuclear war, but since then has been left in peace.

110. TRAMWAY BRIDGE, COYPOOL

Cast iron bowstring bridge over the River Plym built in 1829

The deviation in the route of the Plymouth & Dartmoor Railway which necessitated the tunnel at Leigham brought the line onto land belonging to the Earl of Morley, who lived at Saltram House nearby and was a major landowner. Since an Act of Parliament was required to authorise the deviation from the permitted route, His Lordship saw an opportunity to obtain easy access to the wharves at Sutton Harbour from his slate quarry at Cann Wood, near Plym Bridge. There was already a canal from the quarry to a basin at Marsh Mills, but he indicated that he would not oppose the Bill provided that a branch line from the tramway was built to Cann Quarry, and the Directors felt they had to agree.

But they were short of capital. As an interim measure a line was built in 1829 deviating from the Plymouth & Dartmoor at Marsh Mills, crossing the Plym at Coypool by means of this cast iron bowstring bridge and running a short distance to the canal basin of the Cann Quarry Canal. Four years later, in 1833, the line was extended up the Plym Valley along what is now the Plym Valley Trail to the quarry. This was an easy route, as much of the track could be laid along the towpath of the canal.

There was also a short-lived branch to Plympton, which ran from near this bridge along the north side of Plymouth Road as far as St Mary's Bridge. This was built to enable china clay brought down from Lee Moor in horse-drawn wagons to be carried by rail to the wharves at Cattedown. It opened in 1834, but closed in 1847 because the broad gauge South Devon Railway from Exeter cut the branch in two, and the Directors' objections failed to prevent Parliament from approving the necessary Bill.

This left the clay works at Lee Moor without rail access to the wharves at Cattedown. On this occasion Lord Morley proved to be of service to the Plymouth & Dartmoor, as he agreed with the South Devon Railway that he would not oppose them provided they paid for the cost of building a tramway from Lee Moor down to the Plym Valley, where it would join the Cann Quarry branch.

The Lee Moor Tramway opened in 1854 and survived until 1960. It left the Cann Quarry line at Plym Bridge, where the stables for the horses can still be seen beside the walking trail. From there it climbed through Cann Woods by means of a 1¼ mile rope-worked incline, then ran through fields and across the Wotter Brook to the Torycombe china clay works, where there was another rope-worked incline up to Lee Moor. From there it connected with a number of clay pits as far west as Cholwichtown. This upper section was worked by steam locomotives, which have been preserved.

Until 1960 the incongruous sight of ancient clay wagons hauled along the Embankment by slowly plodding carthorses while main line express trains whooshed past, continued to delight those fortunate enough to see it.

111. PEREGRINE FALCON WATCH, CANN WOODS

The dedicated team of watchers who protect the nesting peregrines

Peregrines are the country's largest falcons, with a wingspan of about 4 feet. They are among the fastest creatures in the world, reaching speeds of up to 200 miles an hour when swooping down on their prey from far above. They take medium-sized birds like pigeons, doves and small ducks.

Although they are not an endangered species, peregrines are a Schedule 1 listed species under the Wildlife & Countryside Act. They are not popular with those who rear game birds or keep racing pigeons, and despite protection they are sometimes killed. They also suffer from the unwelcome attention of birds' egg collectors.

Peregrine falcons have been raising young at Cann Quarry near Plym Bridge for at least 50 years. The Plym Peregrine Project was started in 2001 under the aegis of the National Trust following the deliberate poisoning of the birds in 2000, and since then teams of volunteers keep watch over the resident falcons from March through to fledging in late June/July and beyond. Since the project started, some 35 chicks have successfully left the nest, and some of the young have been recorded at other locations, raising their own chicks. The chicks are ringed so that their movements can be followed for research and conservation purposes once they have left the nest. How one rings a chick when it is on a small ledge halfway up a sheer quarry face protected by angry falcons is something the volunteers will no doubt be able to explain to you.

The Plym Peregrine Project site lies on the route of the Plym Valley Trail (also part of the West Devon Way). This starts at Coypool near the Park & Ride, and following the course of the old Cann Quarry tramway, runs alongside the Plym Valley Steam Railway as far as Plym Bridge. Here the steam railway ends, and from there on the trail follows that of the former Great Western branch line towards Tavistock and Launceston, running up the wooded Plym and Meavy valleys, now high up on lofty viaducts, now passing through dense groves of oak, ash and sycamore.

At the viewing platform you can borrow binoculars or telescopes so you can see the birds and their nest, perched on a crevice in the vertical quarry face. Cann Viaduct provides an ideal viewpoint, as the nest is more or less at eye level, and depending where the birds choose to nest you may be watching from as little as 200 yards away. If you are lucky, you will see them flying to head off an intruder, or just enjoying the freedom of flight. Once the chicks are ready, the parents will encourage them to fly, and teach them how to hunt prey for themselves.

Apart from protecting the nesting birds while they are at their most vulnerable, the aim of the project is to educate and inspire visitors to the area, and to show children from local schools and clubs the range of wildlife to be seen on their doorstep.

112. SALTRAM PARK AND HARDWICK WOOD

Open parkland, estuary views and ancient woodland

Plymouth has a wealth of parkland, and much of it is featured elsewhere in this guide. Just as the landscaped park at Mount Edgcumbe lies to the west across the Tamar, so to the east lies Saltram Park. This was also laid out in the 18th century, and although not so fine as that at Mount Edgcumbe, includes follies and undulating parkland with groves of trees, and makes for a pleasant walk.

There is a good walk to be had around Saltram Park and nearby Hardwick Wood. The walk is about 5 miles (depending which of many paths you take through Hardwick Wood) and takes three hours or so. From the car park at the entrance to Chelson Meadow Recycling Centre there is a new walkway along The Ride through groves of hornbeam and thorn to the Quay at Saltram Point. The walk continues alongside the Plym estuary with glimpses through the leaves of estuarial birds and the occasional passing train. Here on your right there is well-established woodland with some fine beeches and oaks, while on your left, leaning out over the mudflats, are the scrub oak trees which are such a feature of the South Devon estuaries.

The walk takes you past the Amphitheatre which the Parkers built in the 1740s, a circle of lawn jutting out into the estuary with a classical archway looking down onto it. Although this looks from a distance like a grand entrance to the estate, in fact it is only a folly, with a blank wall behind it. The Amphitheatre was made for entertaining the family's guests with fireworks and dancing.

Further on is a bird 'hide' that offers a good view of the ducks and geese in the salt marshes. Then the woodland ends and the path divides, with the left hand path leading to Coypool and Plym Valley Trail, and the right hand path climbing up to the car park for Saltram House and garden. Here you continue uphill to the woods and Stag Lodge, a pair of single-storey stone lodges designed by Robert Adam, where a short walk along the road over the A38 brings you to Hardwick Wood. The entrance is a short way downhill.

Hardwick Wood is maintained by the Woodland Trust, and is one of their top ten bluebell woods, "a must-visit in the spring time for anyone looking to admire the swathes of brilliant bluebells which cover the woodland floor". It has a wealth of woodland flowers and wildlife. When we visited in early May 2020 there was a carpet of wild garlic stretching as far as one could see, and up above, a Concerto for Blackbirds (with Distant Cuckoo). Quite magical.

Some years ago a young lad buzzing around on his 50cc moped entered the wood and met with a phantom, a 'shimmering white figure' which he could see through. He could never be persuaded to go back. Other unrelated sightings have been made in the area too, and dogs are occasionally reluctant to enter.

There are many paths in the wood, and care should be taken to ensure you do a circular walk back to the entrance. On your return it is possible to take a shortcut to Saltram Point along the tarred road running down the valley.

113. PLYMPTON ST MARY'S CHURCH

A fine 14th century church with a remarkably well-preserved tomb from 1461

There are some fine old churches in the Plymouth area, but the finest is undoubtedly this one, completed in 1311 by the monks of Plympton Priory, in whose grounds it stands.

A monastery was established here by 904, by the son of Alfred the Great. It appears that over the following 200 years the monks got into bad habits, since in 1121 it was re-established by the Bishop of Exeter as an Augustinian priory because the monks 'had refused to give up their concubines'. The Priory became extremely powerful and wealthy, owning large tracts of land all over Devon and parts of Cornwall, including most of the area covered by modern day Plymouth and even parts of Exeter. The Black Prince (the son of Edward III) was entertained here by the Prior in 1348 after returning from France.

Up to the thirteenth century the creek was navigable right up to the Priory buildings, and pilgrims would embark here for the great pilgrimage to Santiago de Compostela in Spain. They could be a rowdy lot, and the monks provided accommodation for them well away from the serenity of the cloister, in what is now part of the church's Lady Katherine Chapel.

By the time of the Dissolution of the Monasteries under King Henry VIII it was one of the richest in the country. The Priory buildings were all swept away in 1539, and only a few walls survive.

The most striking thing about the church's exterior is the massive tower, which rises 91 feet to the battlements, with a turret and pinnacle at each corner in the local style.

Inside, there is much of interest to be seen, including an unusual chair of 'scrimshaw' work (carving in wood or ivory, typically carried out by sailors on whaling ships to pass the time during long voyages), and the exquisite choir stalls of 1898 carved by the Pinwill Sisters of Plymouth.

Perhaps the gems are the two Strode family monuments in the Lady Katherine Chapel. High on the north wall is the memorial to Sir William Strode of 1637, with his two wives and their seven daughters and three sons. The sculptor shows Sir William kneeling in prayer and in the full flow of oratory, flanked by his bored-looking wives who appear to have heard it all before.

To the left of the chapel altar is the tomb of Richard Strode of Newnham, who died in 1461, the year when the Yorkists defeated the Lancastrians in the Wars of the Roses and Edward IV deposed Henry VI. The state of preservation of the stonework and the detail of the armour is remarkable for a 560-year-old monument. The fact that his descendant Sir Richard Strode was a puritan who supported Parliament in the Civil War when Plympton was a Royalist stronghold, makes its condition all the more surprising. It is possible that his family concealed the tomb behind a false wall until the risk of damage had passed.

114. PLYMPTON CASTLE

Norman motte and bailey castle, and Plympton's past glory

We tend to think that Plymouth, Plympton and Plymstock were all named after the River Plym, but it appears that the river was named after the towns and not the other way round. The earliest reference to Plympton is as 'Plementun' (believed to be from the Old English for 'Plum Tree Farm') in an Anglo-Saxon charter of about 900 AD. So far as Plymstock is concerned, the Domesday Book of 1086 refers to it as 'Plemestocha', which also means 'Plum Tree Farm' but implies that it was an outlying farmstead of Plympton.

In Saxon times a wooden fort was built here to protect the wealthy monastery from raids by the Danes. The present motte and bailey castle was built in about 1100 after the Norman Conquest. A motte is a raised mound or earthwork with a fortified tower of stone or timber on top which served as the defensive keep, and a bailey is the area around the motte, enclosed and protected by a ditch and a palisade of wooden stakes. These castles were relatively simple to build, and if enough slaves, serfs and villeins were available, they could be finished in a few weeks.

A fourteenth century drawing of Plympton Castle shows a circular stone tower about thirty feet high on the motte. The living quarters and storerooms would have been wooden buildings in the bailey. The bailey was surrounded by a moat, with access via a fortified gatehouse and drawbridge.

The castle was besieged twice by the monarchy. In 1136 the Earl of Devon, Baldwin de Redvers, rebelled against King Stephen, who sent knights and archers to take Plympton and subdue the castle. It was later rebuilt.

In 1224 a subsequent owner of the castle, Fawkes de Breaute, rebelled against King Henry III. The King sent the Sheriff of Devon to attack the castle with a strong force including three siege-engines, and the castle surrendered after fifteen days. These local rebellions often arose because of resentment over financial demands by the King, who raised money for wars by taxing the manors, or because of disputes over land.

During the Civil War, Plympton was held by the Royalists and the castle was used as a base by Prince Maurice in 1643 to support the siege of Plymouth. After he was forced to withdraw in 1644 following the Sabbath Day Fight at Freedom Fields, the castle fell into ruin. By this time, Plympton had ceased to be an important town. The Priory had long gone. The tidal creek from the River Plym at Marsh Mills had silted up because of mining waste and was no longer navigable, and trade had moved downstream to Plymouth.

Parts of the castle wall remain on top of the motte, accessible via the original winding pathway, and the bailey remains an open space for recreation and fairs, including the annual Lamb Feast.

115. PLYMPTON GRAMMAR SCHOOL

Listed school building of 1671 and birthplace of the artist Joshua Reynolds

Plympton Grammar School was founded by Mr Elize Hele of Cornwood, a lawyer and philanthropist who left money for charitable purposes. The school opened in 1671, with a big schoolroom over a rather Venetian-looking arcade of striped stone, and other rooms adjoining.

Joshua Reynolds was born in 1723, the seventh of eleven children of the Master of the school, the Reverend Samuel Reynolds, and his wife Theophila. Five of their children died in infancy, and Joshua himself suffered from smallpox at some stage (he recovered but remained disfigured by it). The Master's house where they lived was replaced in 1869 by the present house next to the school. Samuel Reynolds was not without influence, being on familiar terms with both the Parkers of Saltram and Lord Edgcumbe.

Sir Joshua Reynolds is one of the most well-regarded British portrait painters of the eighteenth century. As a young man he was encouraged by a family friend, the philosopher and clergyman Zachariah Mudge, and he read widely from the classics as well as works on the theory of art.

When he was 17, Reynolds was apprenticed to the fashionable London portrait painter Thomas Hudson, who had been born in Devon. He then worked on his own as a portrait painter in Plymouth Dock, sharing a house with his sisters, and it would have been there that he painted the portrait opposite, showing himself aged 24. Here he was introduced to Commodore Keppel, who invited him to join him on HMS *Centurion* on a voyage to the Mediterranean, calling at Lisbon, Cádiz and the Balearic Islands. From Minorca he travelled to Livorno and then to Rome, where he spent two years studying the Old Masters and acquiring a taste for the 'Grand Style'.

On his return Reynolds rapidly became one of London's most fashionable portrait painters. He was the first President of the Royal Academy of Arts, and was knighted in 1769 (a rare honour for an artist). He even became the King's 'Principal Painter in Ordinary' at his own request, although he found the position uncongenial, complaining to his friend James Boswell: "If I had known what a shabby, miserable place it is, I would not have asked for it".

Reynolds also founded The Club, an association of leading intellectuals including Samuel Johnson, James Boswell and David Garrick.

To us, his work seems sometimes to veer between the inspired and the insipid. While some of his contemporaries, such as William Blake, mocked him for painting people in poses borrowed from the works of earlier masters, others admired him for his instinct for colour and composition, and his ability to capture the sitter's personality. He died in 1792 and was buried in St Paul's Cathedral. The great J M W Turner admired him and his work so much that he asked to be interred at his side.

116. DIVING MUSEUM, YACHT HAVEN QUAY

Davy Jones' locker with salvaged collection of underwater treasures

Ray Ives' diving museum is as unusual as Ray himself, containing diving equipment and marine artefacts collected over the course of a long and varied life as a deep-sea diver. It was opened by the broadcaster and marine biologist Monty Halls in 2013.

Ray was born in 1936 and joined the Royal Marines when he was 17, spending twelve years as a Green Beret serving in Egypt, Malaysia and Borneo. When he was discharged in 1965 he got work as a diver at Devonport Dockyard, and diving became his passion. He worked for a time with a salvage company before the oil boom of the 1970s drew him to Scotland, where he was diving from oil rigs and laying undersea pipelines at depths of 600 feet.

He was one of the first divers in the country to do saturation diving, a very specialized form of diving which changed the way deep sea diving was carried out. In saturation diving, divers live in a pressurized environment for several weeks, transferring between underwater living quarters and a pressurised diving bell to return to the working area. This minimises the risk of decompression sickness and the time spent decompressing.

Ray nearly lost his life during a saturation dive off the coast of Norway. Because of incorrectly mixed gas in his tanks he lost consciousness while he was working outside the diving bell, and although his colleague was advised not to go out after him, he found Ray and resuscitated him. It took Ray 40 hours in a decompression chamber to recover, and he was told he might have suffered permanent brain damage. Fortunately he was back at work a month later.

He worked alongside Red Adair for ten months in 1979/80 dealing with the catastrophic 'Ixtoc 1' oil leak in the Bay of Campeche, Mexico. An explosion had caused the largest-ever undersea oil leak, when almost 3.3 million barrels of oil gushed into the sea for nine months until it was brought under control.

His museum is housed in two shipping containers at Yacht Haven Quay. As well as deep sea diving equipment, it has a fascinating and varied collection of weapons - cannonballs and a fine brass cannon, shells, small arms, muskets and rifles – together with bottles, plates, leather and hundreds of clay pipes, all recovered from wrecks and the sea bed.

Plymouth Sound is one of the best places for scuba diving because of the number of wrecks and the easy access to sheltered water. The colour of the marine life is beautiful: "It's like being in a bluebell wood – simply a wonderful sight".

Amanda Bluglass of Plymouth University has produced a 15 minute documentary entitled *Ray - A Life Underwater*, which has been a multi-award winning hit across the globe.

117. MARINE ROAD, ORESTON

Where Alexander Selkirk, the real-life Robinson Crusoe, lived for a time

Alexander Selkirk was born in Fife in 1676. He was a colourful character, who chose a life at sea as a buccaneer, sailing with privateers seeking wealth from prize money by capturing enemy merchant ships. In character he was an argumentative and unruly individual, well suited to the rough and tumble of life at sea. In 1703 he joined a privateering expedition to the South Pacific led by Captain William Dampier, serving as sailing master aboard the vessel Cinque Ports which was accompanying Dampier.

The expedition was dangerous and met with resistance, and the ships sustained damage. When the leaking Cinque Ports stopped at an uninhabited Pacific island called *Más a Tierra* (part of Chile, now called Isla Robinson Crusoe) in 1704 to take on water and supplies, Selkirk and the captain argued whether repairs should be done before going any further. When Selkirk said he would rather stay on the island than continue in a dangerously leaking ship, the captain marooned him there with a musket, a hatchet, a knife, a cooking pot, a Bible, and some bedding and clothes. It was probably little consolation to him that the Cinque Ports later foundered, and many of the crew drowned.

Selkirk proved extremely resourceful, living off wild goats, lobsters, fruits and vegetables, and building separate huts for cooking and sleeping. He tamed some feral cats to keep the rats away, and made himself clothes from goat skins. He was rescued in 1709 by a privateering expedition led by Captain Rogers, who was impressed not only by his remarkable health, but also by the calm acceptance he had shown in coping with his lonely situation. Selkirk joined Rogers' expedition and resumed the life of a privateer with enthusiasm, finally returning to England in 1711.

When an account of his experiences was published by Captain Rogers, Selkirk became a celebrity, and a wealthy one, as his share of the prize money would be worth some £120,000 today. But the lure of the sea held him, and in 1717 he joined the Royal Navy. He was paid off at Plymouth in 1720, and while there he married Frances Candish, the landlady of the Old Inn at Oreston, which stood near Minard's House in Marine Road. But this marriage was extremely short-lived, as after only a few days he was back at sea, serving as Master's Mate aboard HMS *Weymouth* engaged in anti-piracy patrol off the 'fever coast' of West Africa. He died there of yellow fever in 1721.

Alexander Selkirk was the inspiration for *Robinson Crusoe*, the novel by Daniel Defoe published in 1719 about a castaway on a tropical desert island. In many ways the actions of Crusoe mirror those of Selkirk, although Defoe allowed his imagination free rein, introducing the character of Man Friday and encounters with cannibals and mutineers. *Robinson Crusoe* is regarded as the first true 'novel', literary fiction presented as if it were a true story. It is one of the most widely-published books ever, and is said to be second only to the Bible in the number of translations which have been made of it.

118. RADFORD PARK AND HOOE LAKE

Ornamental boating lake with folly castle, and the hulks of Hooe Lake

Radford Park, Hooe, lies in the grounds of the historic Radford House, which like so many great houses was demolished in the 1930s. The house and estate were owned by the Harris family for over 500 years. During the reign of Queen Elizabeth I, Sir Christopher Harris was Plymouth's MP and also Vice-Admiral for Devon, so it was at Radford that the victory celebration for the defeat of the Spanish Armada was held, attended by Francis Drake, Walter Raleigh, Lord Howard of Effingham, John Hawkins, Martin Frobisher and others.

In recognition of his role during the battle, Harris was given the Armada Service, a magnificent collection of twenty-two silver dishes made from silver said to have been captured from Spanish merchant ships. During the Civil War the Harris family hid the collection on Dartmoor to avoid it being seized by the Parliamentarians, but it appears the safe place was too safe, as subsequently they were unable to find it. The collection was eventually found in 1827 by a farm labourer who put his pickaxe through one of the dishes, and it is now in the British Museum.

In the early 1800s Radford Creek was dammed, with a romantic castle by the sluice for the groundsman. An arboretum was created, and a boathouse and a lodge by the entrance to the drive were built, which survive in part.

Below the dam lies Hooe Lake, a tidal inlet off the Cattewater which has been used for trading and ship repairing since before Roman times. It has the largest concentration of hulks west of the Exe estuary. Many of these are so decayed as to be difficult to identify, but a survey by students from Plymouth University found evidence of around 15 abandoned vessels. One of Hooe's best known hulks was the *Shamrock*, a Tamar sailing barge built to carry stone, lime, coal and other goods to the many quays along the tidal stretch of the River Tamar, and to harbours along the coast between Salcombe and Falmouth. Fortunately she was rescued before deterioration had progressed too far, and was rebuilt by the National Trust and National Maritime Museum at Cotehele Quay, where she is now based.

The mudbanks of Hooe Lake contain the remains of another Tamar barge, and a larger vessel, probably the sloop *Pearl* built in the 1880s. Other skeletons include the Brixham trawlers *Wendew* and *Antelope*, both medium-sized beam trawlers, the timber lighter *Arthur*, and the hull bottom of the motor trawler *Roger*.

Hooe Lake, Radford Lake and woods, and Radford Quarry are some of the best areas for wildlife in Devon, and constitute an irreplaceable habitat for many rare and endangered species. The area is designated as a County Wildlife Site. It is a good place to see estuarial and wading birds like herons, oystercatchers, mallards and curlews.

119. TURNCHAPEL WHARVES

Old fishing cove, formerly a base for transatlantic cable ships

Gordon Bennett, the proprietor of the *New York Herald*, often scandalized people with his erratic behaviour. On a visit to England in 1877 he arrived late and drunk at a party, then urinated into a fireplace (some say it was a grand piano) in full view of his hosts. Bennett's controversial reputation is believed to have inspired the phrase 'Gordon Bennett!' as an expression of incredulity.

His link with Turnchapel is that in 1884 he and John Mackay (who had made a fortune as a silver prospector in Nevada) founded the Commercial Cable Company, and launched their cable-laying ship, the *Mackay-Bennett*, so they could compete with the only other cable-laying company and so reduce the cost of transatlantic telegraphy. Undersea cables were vital to Bennett's newspaper empire, and cables had successfully been laid from Nova Scotia to Waterville in Ireland. The *Mackay-Bennett* was later to be one of the vessels which searched for bodies after the *Titanic* sank in 1912.

In 1903 the Admiralty became interested in using submarine cables to detect enemy submarines and to provide a secure communication system. It bought the boatyard at Turnchapel Wharves, which was an ideal site for a cable ship base, with its deep water anchorage and its proximity to Devonport and the open sea. The Commercial Cable Company was already chartering ships to the Admiralty, and in 1922 moved their European base to Turnchapel as well. The ageing *Mackay-Bennett* was moored off the wharves as a storage hulk, and remained there until she was scrapped in 1965, apart from a brief period in 1941 when she was hit by enemy planes and sank at her moorings. She was recovered and underwent repair in the dry dock at Millbay.

Since the earliest days of undersea cables and the pioneering transatlantic cables laid by Brunel's Great Eastern, British seamen and cable ships had led the world in deep sea cable-laying, and this was put to good use during both World Wars. Britain's first action after declaring war on Germany in 1914 was to cut the five cables linking Germany with France, Spain and the Azores, and through them, North America. This left Germany reliant on wireless messaging, which could be monitored by London. In the Second World War, German and Italian cables were dredged up and either diverted for use by the Allies or intercepted. The German cable from Denmark to America was 'tapped' and relayed to Porthcurno Cable Station, and it was some time before German High Command became aware of it.

Turnchapel Cable Ship base continued in operation until 1993, when the wharves became a Royal Marine Assault Squadron base. They are now used as a commercial marine business park. But even in this age of satellite communications, undersea cables remain of the highest importance because of their reliability and high speed, and carry 99% of the data traffic across the oceans. Few are aware of Turnchapel's historic role in this.

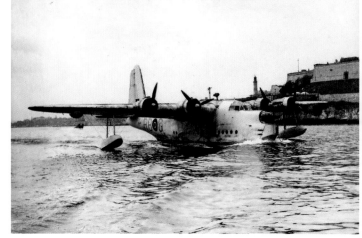

120. FLYING BOAT HANGARS, MOUNT BATTEN

Where flying boats and air-sea rescue craft were maintained for 68 years

The little peninsula at Mount Batten has been many things over the centuries –Bronze Age settlement, Roman trading post, Civil War defensive position, quarry, shipbuilding yard, rifle range and golf course. It is now a water sports centre, with a number of bars and restaurants. But it is best known as an RAF base for flying boats.

A flying boat is (as its name implies) a boat with wings. It has a fuselage adapted for landing on water, while a seaplane is an aeroplane with floats instead of wheels. Both types were stationed here at various times.

The present buildings date from 1917 when Mount Batten was chosen as a site for a seaplane base, and are Grade II listed. It was originally designated RNAS Cattedown. Seaplanes were used to search for U-boats, and were launched and recovered by a steam crane mounted on rails which extended along Mount Batten pier. In 1918 the base was transferred to the newly-formed Royal Air Force, and RAF Mount Batten became an important place for pioneering long-distance flights. In 1927 four Supermarine Southampton flying boats flew from here to Australia, Japan and Singapore, alighting 29 times to refuel.

In 1929 Aircraftman TE Shaw reported for duty. This was none other than the famous secret agent, diplomat and writer Colonel TE Lawrence, better known as Lawrence of Arabia. It appears he wanted a time of reflection after his tumultuous years in the Middle East, insisting on enlisting as an NCO and changing his name in an unsuccessful attempt to avoid publicity. He remained at RAF Mount Batten for four years, working on the early development of high speed rescue boats. He died in a motorcycle accident in 1935.

In 1939, as war clouds gathered over Europe, RAF Mount Batten acquired its first Short Sunderland flying boats. These were as different from the flimsy biplanes which preceded them as swans are from ducks – huge four-engine monoplanes bristling with armaments and carrying radar, searchlights and depth charges. They carried a crew of between seven and eleven, with bunks and cooking facilities to enable them to run 18 hour patrols over the North Atlantic. They proved themselves devastating against U-boats and patrolling German fighters, and when in April 1940 a Sunderland operating off Norway was attacked by six German twin-engine fighters, it shot one down, damaged another sufficiently to force it to land, and drove off the rest.

In November 1940 the hangars were badly damaged by enemy planes, together with two Sunderlands moored in the Cattewater, and the Navy oil tanks at Turnchapel were ignited. Fortunately the Air Ministry tanks were unaffected.

After the war RAF Mount Batten became a base for fast air-sea rescue launches, and aircrews were trained in evacuation from ditched planes. It closed in 1986 together with the Mount Batten weather centre. The hangars are now used by boatyards for yacht maintenance.